PREPOSTEROUS PAPA

PREPOSTEROUS PAPA

by Lewis Meyer

St. Martin's Press
New York

LIBRARY OF CONGRESS CATALOGING-IN-PUBLICATION DATA

Meyer, Lewis

    Preposterous Papa : a hilarious and affectionate portrait by his
son / Lewis Meyer.

      p.   cm.

    ISBN 0-312-08280-0 (pbk.)

    1. Meyer, Lewis, 1913–   —Biography—Family. 2. Authors,
American—20th century—Biography—Family. 3. Fathers and sons-
-United States—Biography. 4. Oklahoma—Social life and customs.
5. Texas—Social life and customs. I. Title.

PS3563.E877Z475   1992

813'.54—dc20

[B]   92-18458

                                               CIP

10 9 8 7 6 5 4 3 2 1

To Natasha, Papa's Daughter-in-Law

CONTENTS

BRIDGING THE YEARS

When one lives a day at a time, the past takes on a new meaning. Yesterday resembles a rubber band. It can be a few hours away, or just as easily it can stretch for years.

Preposterous Papa is a lighthearted book, written yesterday from the viewpoint of a young man about his dynamic, virile, incredible father.

Most of us lead a good part of our lives before we realize that we are becoming mirror images of our own parents. I'm convinced that preposterousness, too, is an inherited trait. At the time I wrote this book, I was unaware that I was saying "Thank you" to Papa for my own preposterous genes.

Now my editor has asked me to write a short additional chapter—he calls it a "retrospective"—and I find myself reliving the day before yesterday all over again, only to discover it has suddenly stretched into today.

I have the most vivid memories of that earlier yesterday

when *Preposterous Papa* was first published. I traveled all over the country autographing books—and Papa kept step with me, affixing his unreadable—Chinese? Cherokee? Hebraic?—surrealist signature to every book that was signed.

He reveled in the book, and he reveled in being something of a local celebrity. He even bought some of those tiny return-address stickers, each one reading "Max Meyer, Preposterous Papa." He stuck them on his letters, of course, but he stuck them in other places I'd rather not mention.

The Saturday Evening Post devoted a good part of two issues to the book. The first week they ran the last chapter. The next, they ran a full account with pictures of the celebration of Preposterous Papa Day in Sapulpa, Oklahoma—with floats, marching bands, and a replica of the famous house that was moved, starring Papa and two Indian friends sitting on the front porch (which was really the back porch because it was being towed). It was Papa's Day and the crowds who hollered "Give 'em hell, Max!" were his personal friends who loved and respected him all of their lives.

When the book was optioned for a TV series Papa was transported. When a movie based on the book was optioned he couldn't contain himself. When all options were dropped he said only, "Just you wait, Sonny Boy. Some day ... Some day ..."

My children called him Opa. Opa spoiled them with continuous presents. He spoiled everybody. He bestowed gifts of his "natural stone" on half of Sapulpa. We still have the walk-ways and garden trims from the dozens of pieces of "natural stone" he brought us. After all, he had hundreds of acres of "natural stone," which he considered the *ne plus ultra* of building materials. He gave Chinese Ellums to anyone who wanted them. He still had thousands and thousands of unsold ones in his nursery, getting bigger and bigger every day. And barbecue sauce! People still stop me on the street to tell me of their gift of barbecue sauce (which was really firewater!). One person put it this way: "He always cautioned us to use one part of his sauce to ten parts of ketchup, but it still blew our heads off!"

Once, I said to my father, "Papa, don't you ever get depressed? You just smile and laugh all the time."

His answer shouldn't have startled me, but it did. "Sonny Boy, I'm smiling for God, because God has smiled on me."

God had indeed smiled on him, and had blessed him with oil royalties of a thousand dollars a day for four full years— before the income tax! Other than to accumulate more land, he never invested a penny of his windfall. He just spent it. And that's what the book is about. There may be doubters, but I will swear that every word in the book is the truth: the five-acre lake excavated from a blueprint, the 100,000 Chinese Ellums, the tourist courts on both sides of Highway 66 "to catch people coming and going." Oh yes! and the silos: three huge red brick silos, not one of which ever had a foot of silage in it. "People criticize me for them silos," he confided, "but they don't consider how pretty and red and tall they are—and how the airplanes sight on them when they fly over." All these were his gadgets, his joy.

"Sonny Boy," he said to me more than once, "I know people say I'm foolish for throwing money around like a crazy man, but where would I have invested it? Both Sapulpa banks went broke and I'd lost it there. The stock market crashed and

I'd lost it there. At least I have the land to show for some of it. And there's more oil there, too. Plenty of it. You'll see." And then he added his own version of the Living Trust before there was a Living Trust: "If you ever sell the land, sell only the surface. Keep all the oil rights. Remember: keep all the oil rights!"

I remember saying to him, "Papa, it's your money. You don't have to make excuses to anybody. Enjoy it." I meant it then and I still mean it.

Papa never mentioned the generous way he had invested in his own children. He gave us the best of educations, the best horses to ride, the best tennis courts to play on, the best (certainly the largest) swimming pool.

It's only fair to say that after Papa was gone and all the lands were sold we remembered his advice of selling only the surface. *"Sell only the surface. Keep all the oil rights."* We kept all the oil rights.

I understand what the poet meant when he wrote, "The child is father to the man." God smiled again on my father when he presented him with his personal ambulatory money machine.

"Sonny Boy, I need fifty cents." I knew he was going to spend it on raw vegetables for his lunch at the Farmers Exchange.

In the same tone of voice he'd say, "Sonny Boy, I need ten thousand dollars." This request came at the depth of the Depression. The taxes were due, and the other children were giving me Hail Columbia for giving Papa whatever he asked for.

As I was writing out the check I did inquire, "Papa,

whatever is the ten thousand dollars for?"

He beamed. "I've got to build an island in the lake."

"An *island?*"

"Yes. The grandchildren need an island to row around when they are in the boat. An island is so . . . scenic."

The island was built. And by golly it *was* scenic.

Papa liked figures. Big figures. "Sonny Boy, the oil runs only make thirty thousand dollars a month. A person can't tackle anything *big* with thirty thousand dollars—but with a *hundred thousand*—ahhhhh. A man can really *do things* with a hundred thousand!"

So I took Papa's oil runs to the Tulsa bank and pledged them and borrowed $100,000 at a time (with 10 percent interest), and he started doing things immediately. He bought 580 steel frames to enclose the entire open porch–dining area, he bought a new Cadillac for each of his children (I was fourteen years old and a senior at Sapulpa High School, with a seven-passenger Cadillac of my own, from which at least twelve people were always hanging out of the various orifices.) He bought the latest electric milkers for the new dairy barn, he started work on five new humongous barbecue pits—all essential gadgets. That was the time he conceived tearing out the existing fireplaces in the ranch house and constructing three new ones, a fireplace for each floor.

The original editor of this book refused to let me tell many of Papa's antics. His grounds were "no one would believe they really happened." I was hurt when he threw out the part I'd written about Papa's lawsuit. When a trucking company sued Papa for damages he had inflicted when he crashed into the back of one of its large trucks, Papa countersued—and requested a jury trial. The damages for the trucking company were disallowed. Papa was awarded in full the cost of his car. This resourceful man had created a new kind of military maneuver known as the Sudden Attack from the Rear! Of course it really happened. Who in the world could invent a preposterous story like that?

He was eighty-four when we clandestinely suggested that the highway patrol remove his driver's license. He had been leaving his imprint on at least two fenders a day. The proximate cause of our action was Papa's arrest for driving the wrong way on the bypass—in the rain.

He was officially booked and his hearing date set for 10:00 A.M. in Judge Luther Lane's court. Papa, trying mightily to appear chastened, was sitting by me when the case of Highway Patrol vs. Max Meyer was announced by the bailiff.

Judge Lane, who had seemed comatose until that moment, suddenly sat up straight in his padded chair and said, "Max Meyer? Did I hear Max Meyer? Will Max Meyer please stand up?"

Papa looked at me. "Stand up, Papa," I said.

"Aren't you the Max Meyer we know as Preposterous Papa?"

"Yes, Your Honor," Papa answered, summoning his last ounce of humility as he sent a subdued smile at the judge.

Judge Lane was visibly excited. "I want everyone in this courtroom to stand and pay tribute to a man who symbolizes the pioneers who made Oklahoma the great state it is because they *thought big!*"

The patrolman jumped up, protesting, "But Judge! This man was going the wrong way on the bypass. The *wrong wa—*"

"Shut up!" Judge Lane commanded. "I rule Preposterous Papa *not guilty*. Case dismissed. You can go home now, Max."

The spectators were still standing as I escorted my father from the courtroom.

—Lewis Meyer
Tulsa, Oklahoma
May 1992

INTRODUCTION

Two things in this book are absolutely real. One is Sapulpa. The other is Papa.

Sapulpa is the name of the town in Oklahoma where Papa settled in 1906, shortly before statehood. Sapulpa is a pleasant community which nestles in the shadow of the ever-growing metropolis that is Tulsa, yet maintains an identity and character of its own.

And Papa is as real as Sapulpa. There is no temptation to enlarge him. He is bigger than life. What may seem incredible is true—his lake, his silos, his flagpole, his forest of elms, even the number of his gallstones.

The names and identities of most of the other characters in this story have been changed, for they are not intended to represent real people. They are meant instead to be composites or symbols of the many people who inhabited Papa's world. For there are many men like Papa who have

9

lived exciting and fantastic lives in Oklahoma. As the frontier disappears these colorful citizens are gone forever, but it is men like them—and not their more conventional offspring—who inspire books.

When I told Papa that I had, in fact, written a book about him, he received the news with quiet dignity. I think he said, "That's real nice of you, Sonny," and mumbled, "Don't know who'd want to read a book about me. I'm not the book type." But this modestly subdued behavior lasted for only two days. The morning of the third day he came to my house early.

"Have a cup of coffee, Papa?" I asked.

"No, thanks," he said as he walked nervously around the room, whacking his thigh with some typing paper he was carrying in a roll. His pockets were bulging with notes.

"Sit down, Papa."

He shook his head and kept pacing. "There's no time to sit, Sonny. There's too much to do."

"Do?"

He nodded emphatically. "As soon as you finish your breakfast I want you to get me a stenographer . . . a *first-class* stenographer . . . the sooner the better . . . and be sure she can take dictation—*fast!*"

"But Papa," I said as gently as I could, "the book is already written."

Papa may still write his own book one day. But until he does, I hope that this volume will represent as accurate, as humorous, and as affectionate an account as any one man can write about his own father.

PREPOSTEROUS PAPA

1. WHO IS MAX MEYER?

Turning Papa loose in Oklahoma, Indian Territory, in 1906, was like taking a house cat that had never known more than a corner of a kitchen and letting it run wild in an acre of catnip. Mama's family in Texas had bottled him up until neither he nor they could take each other. Suddenly he was free to call his shots in a new country where every settler had an equal chance. Overnight, Max Meyer blew the cork out of the bottle that had restrained him, and grew into a giant of a man.

Papa fell in love with the confusion that existed on every street and in every building in Sapulpa. He took on the friendly braggadocio of the natives, who were newcomers a month before. The constantly changing scene excited him. "Wait a minute," he'd say. "If your wagon gets stuck in the mud today, wait a minute; the street'll be paved by tomorrow noon."

Things happened almost that quickly. Sidewalks grew. Buildings shot up. Houses appeared. Men followed their impulses and made—or lost—fortunes "in a minute." Nothing was normal, average. Everything was accelerated in pace and exaggerated in size. "Stick a seed into the ground," Papa would say, "and then jump back before you get knocked plumb over by what you planted!" By the same token, you could stick a driller's bit into the earth, then run like fury so you wouldn't get drenched with oil.

Mama ached for Texas. For her, this new country was too bewildering a change from easygoing, tree-shaded Levy Avenue. She forced herself to adjust to the racket and the crowds of new faces, but she sat down and cried about the dust. There were three kinds. The black dust blew in from freshly graded roads across cornfields which yielded their new harvests of derricks and tanks and pipe lines. The red dust blew in from the soft red clay regions. Mama could almost do battle with these two enemies on even terms. But the thin gray dust that came from no place in particular and settled upon just-washed clothes and just-polished furniture defeated her. She fought it with locked windows, with rags stuffed into door casings, with sighs and expletives. Finally she yielded, and taking a lesson from her neighbors, she ignored it. With a resigned, automatic gesture she shook everything vigorously before using it—every piece of clothing, every bedspread, every towel, every tablecloth. She wrapped her breads and rolls and cakes in cheesecloths and hid them inside dresser drawers to keep the dust from finding them.

When Papa heard his bride complaining tearfully about the dust, he kissed her tenderly, lifted her off her feet, and cradled her in his arms, whispering to her reassuringly as you would whisper to a child. "So it's dusty, honey? A little dust never hurt anybody. And for all the dust around here, Oklahoma's got Texas backed off the map for excitement!"

Their favorite stroll was to the top of Sugar Loaf Hill after dark. From this high point they could see miracles in all directions. Cities of lights blinked hesitantly where the clusters of drill stems gouged the earth for sand samplings. Every derrick blazed lights in an L shape, from the top of the rig to the rear of the powerhouse—not the bright even glare one expects today, but lights whose juice came from individual, erratic generators. The yellowish uneven lights lent an incandescent dustiness to the night, matching the choking dustiness of the day. Each well was its own noise factory. The standard drilling tools clanged against hundreds of feet of pipe as they bit their way downward, a foot at a time. At night these oil-field sounds became a kind of frenzy. Standing on the hilltop with Papa, holding tightly to his hand, Mama understood what it was about Oklahoma that thrilled him so much.

Houses were at a premium in Sapulpa. Papa and Mama were lucky to find a modest frame residence for rent on Cedar Street. Papa never stopped being sentimental over this house. He always stopped the car when he drove by it and said to us, "See that house? It's where your mother and I lived when she was expectin' your sister Beatrice.

Only property I ever rented in my life. I never liked to rent; I liked to own. It's small, but it's built solid! Just you wait! The day will come when I buy that house for memory's sake! We loved every minute of the time we lived there, but I was in a big hurry to finish the house on Oak Street and move in. I didn't want my first child gettin' its start in life in a rented house!"

Bea was spared this stigma. Mama moved into the house on Oak Street two months before her baby was born. Where the Cedar Street place had been compact and functional, the new house on Oak Street rambled over two city lots. "Why so many rooms, Max?" Papa was asked by relatives who came to visit. "Well," he explained, "our first baby was on its way before we'd been married a year. I figured we'd be repeatin' pretty regularly. I didn't have time to keep addin' rooms, so I sorta estimated my needs in advance and built it to accommodate an even dozen."

Papa would have loved a child in every room. He wanted lots of children. You could tell this the way he'd say "only four" when someone asked him how many he had. In Papa's heterogeneous collection of medical facts and theories was the notion that a pregnant woman should get a lot of exercise, and there must have been something to his theory. He walked Mama over half the county four times and pointed to four healthy children. Mama liked to remind him that she barely made it back in time to have Manny in her own bed. Papa had hiked her half way to Kiefer when the alarm sounded, and he had to

WHO IS MAX MEYER?

borrow a horse and buggy to get her home before Manny arrived.

During his first months in Oklahoma, Papa spent most of his days campaigning for customers for his store in much the same way that a politician goes out after votes. Like a good politician, he aimed his appeal at the grass roots. He drove his horse and buggy down every road, lane, and driveway in Creek County, pausing only long enough to tack signs on trees, fences, barns, telephone poles, and outhouses. The signs all said the same thing:

WHO IS MAX MEYER?

Sometimes he'd stand by a sign, waiting for the farmer to amble up, read it, and ask, "Who the heck is this here Max Meyer?" Then Papa would introduce himself, and a customer was born.

He'd return from his excursions sunburned, tired, and strangely excited. Riding and walking over the countryside awakened a desire in him to accumulate land for himself. This desire grew into a passion, then turned into an obsession. He wanted more and more. He was always in financial hot water because he'd buy land he couldn't pay for, but couldn't resist. Somehow he managed to hang onto it all— even to the hundreds of acres he bought from maps, without having the vaguest notion where it was located or what it looked like. What he couldn't afford himself he talked his relatives into buying.

"You're greedy, Max," Philip Levy, his wealthy father-in-law, once said to him. "Greedy for land."

"Not greedy," Papa answered with a grin. "I don't want much. Only the eighty acres that join what I already own."

"Is that all?" Philip Levy asked, half amused, half provoked at his son-in-law.

"Not quite. Take that two hundred and forty acres I was tellin' you about this mornin'. I'd like that piece, but I haven't the money to buy it. Haven't even the money to steal it. I swear it's a steal for two thousand dollars. Sure it's rocky, but it's *land* . . . and for less than ten dollars an acre! Buy it. You'll never be sorry."

When Philip Levy returned to Taro, Texas, with a deed to that 240-acre rock pile, his sons snickered. "Max Meyer made a sucker out of you," they hooted. In just a few weeks the Levys made back their purchase price from an oil and gas lease. Within a year there were half a dozen oil wells spaced among the rocks.

"Bless their hearts," Papa said grimly. "They were so grateful they sent me a necktie for my birthday!"

His own father was a tougher nut to crack. Simon Meyer disliked his son's silliness over land and was vocal in his opposition. He wrote many times to Mama urging her to make Papa stop buying land. When this strategy failed, he made special trips to Oklahoma from Arkansas to plead with his son. "Max, you've got a good business. Your customers are taking the merchandise away from you. But you're never there. Stop running around the country buying land like a damned fool. Stay in your store and you'll get rich."

Once Grandpa Meyer came for a visit when Papa was desperately trying to scrape up enough money to "steal" an eight-hundred-acre tract he had had his eye on for three years. Knowing he couldn't swing the deal himself, Papa urged his father to buy it rather than see it go to a stranger.

"Nix, Max," Grandpa Meyer insisted. "I don't believe in owning land. I like buildings and stores. Buildings bring rent and stores bring income. Land brings taxes. I don't want your crazy land at any price."

Papa wouldn't give up. He didn't stop talking about his bargain until his father's resistance wilted. No one was more surprised than Grandpa Meyer when the deed to the tract was handed over to him as the new owner. "I must have been out of my mind," he said.

As time went by, Grandpa Meyer referred to this land as "Max's lemon." Each fall he'd make the trip to Oklahoma to pay taxes on the eight-hundred-acre lemon. He'd never miss an opportunity to complain about his investment. With increased vehemence, he drummed his gospel into Papa's head: "Give up one or the other, Max. Either sell the lands or sell the store. You'll go broke trying to hold onto both of them." Eventually, Grandpa Meyer's advice turned into an ultimatum. "I'm not fooling, Max. If you don't sell the lands *or* the store during my lifetime, you'll not get a thing from me when I'm gone. Make your choice."

Papa couldn't make his choice. He might have wanted to, but he couldn't do it. Simon Meyer was a man of his word. He bequeathed his son five dollars. "I am strongly tempted to leave Max his eight-hundred-acre lemon," his will stated, "but I shall spare him the annual tax burden of throwing good money after bad." What a pity that

Grandpa Meyer didn't yield to his temptation. The eight hundred acres produced more than a quarter of a million dollars in oil royalties for Simon Meyer's heirs.

"I didn't even get a necktie from 'em," Papa quipped. He wasn't bitter about being left out. That he had been right all the time was the important thing to him.

The WHO IS MAX MEYER signs paid off. Business boomed. People came for miles to trade at Papa's store. Believing in signs, Papa let himself go on a new one. He designed a huge banner five feet high and a hundred feet long which extended across the entire front of his store building. This sign proclaimed modestly:

MAX MEYER, OUTFITTER TO MANKIND

You didn't just buy *clothes* from Papa. You bought blarney, hoopla, friendly philosophy, and a floor show. He was always "throwing something in." You never bought a handkerchief in his store. You got it for nothing. Buy a pair of shoes and he'd throw in a new pair of socks. Buy a suit and take your pick from the suspenders rack. "Save your sales tickets," he'd say. "They're good for valuable premiums for the little lady." He had a way of saying "valuable" which made it sound like liquid gold. His premium department contained sets of dishes, clocks, table-cloths, toys, hand-painted trays, water-tumbler-and-pitcher sets, and many other attractive inducements to keep his customers buying.

When a driller brought in a well he'd barge into the store and buy a suit for every member of his crew. If he stopped by to let Papa know that the well was dry, he'd leave with a new Stetson hat on his head—Papa's standard consolation prize for oilmen.

When a customer passed along the information that his wife was expecting a baby, Papa'd say, "If it's a boy bring him in when he's ready for his first suit of clothes. It'll be on the house."

"And if it's a girl?"

"Try again."

A whole generation of boy children in Creek County got their first suits from Max Meyer. It was good advertising and it was good fun. Every time Papa saw Joe Bailey he'd holler, "The offer's over, Joe! Don't try it again!" Then Papa would tell with gusto how he had made his standard deal to Joe about a free suit if it was a boy, and how Joe had come through with twin boys—twice! "Good way to go broke!" Papa would complain, wishing all the time it'd been triplets.

Papa looked like an Indian. Traveling salesmen always asked him what tribe he belonged to. "The Lost Tribe," he'd answer with just enough of a straight face to throw them for a loss. Papa's store in fact was unofficial head-quarters for the Five Civilized Tribes. Indians liked him and trusted him. More than one merchant said, "Get an Indian drunk and you can sell him anything." Papa worked on another theory: get an Indian sober and he'll be your friend. Many Indians came to Papa's store when their money was gone and their hangovers were coming on. Indian women, in their blankets of bright, beautiful colors, spent hours in the shoe department while their men slept off their binges on cots Papa installed for that purpose in a corner of his Bargain Basement.

In his store safe he kept Indians' marriage licenses, army discharges, car registrations, and often considerable sums of cash. He was proud that the Indians trusted him more than they did the bank.

Papa spoke some Creek and understood a little Osage, but he had the know-how of communicating with all the tribes. "I know all the words I need to know," he said. "I know the words for 'drunk,' 'cramp,' 'wife,' 'car,' and 'home.' That's all the vocabulary you need. You can say whatever else has to be said with sign language."

Papa loved the Indians as much as they liked him. He admired their philosophy, even when it boomeranged on him.

"Y'know Henry Whitebird? Know all I've done for Henry? Well, don't forget this story I'm gonna tell you about Henry Whitebird because it explains a lot about Indians.

"Henry used to come to the store when he was broke and I'd give him money to get home on. When he'd get drunk and fight with his wife, I'd hide him so's the police couldn't find him. Once he got careless and . . . uh . . . well, he got . . . 'sick.' His wife would've scalped him if she'd known it wasn't a kidney stone that had Henry on the abstinence list. I got old Doc Eldredge to give Henry treatments until he was . . . uh . . . 'well.' I did a thousand things for Henry Whitebird, and Henry cut my throat. He sold an eighty-acre piece of land that joined my ranch to a feller that turned around and charged me double for it.

When I saw Henry I was fightin' mad. I said, 'Henry, after all I've done for you, how could you pull a trick like that on me? I'd have paid you more for that eighty acres than anyone else and you knew it. Look what I've done for you! Things money couldn't buy!' Henry looked at me without moving a muscle and said, 'I didn't *ask* you to.' "

Then Papa "pointed the moral."

"If you go out of your way to help somebody, that's O.K. But don't expect any favors in return. Remember this, and you'll never get hurt."

One day Sandy Wolfe came into the store to buy a suit. I heard Papa say, "Sandy, that's a good-lookin' diamond ring you're wearin'."

Without hesitation, Sandy took off the ring and handed it to Papa. "Max. Present," he said.

If I was stunned at what I saw, I was even more stunned at Papa's matter-of-fact acceptance of the ring. He put it on his finger, thanked Sandy, and proceeded to sell him a suit.

When Sandy was at the front door ready to leave, Papa said casually, "Sandy, I'm grateful for your generosity, but I forgot to tell you I can't wear rings on my fingers. They hurt me. Please take it back with my thanks. You are a good friend."

After Sandy had replaced the ring on his finger and gone, I said, "Gee, Pop, you gave it *back!*"

"Of course, Son. I've been presented with everything from Cadillac cars to papooses. Indians give you things when they like you. Only you're supposed to give them back after a little while."

"What if you *hadn't* given him back the ring?"

"Are you crazy?" Papa said, his eyes narrowing. "I want to keep on bein' Sandy Wolfe's friend. He's a nice, quiet-talkin' feller all right, but I saw him kill two men in cold blood right in front of my store. He had his reasons for doin' it, and maybe they were good reasons. He pleaded self-defense at the trial and went scot-free. I was his character witness."

"Gee, Papa, I'd have given the ring back, too!"

One of Papa's steadiest friends was an unsteady behemoth of an Indian woman named Wassie Guineahen. This kind of name was not an uncommon one in those days. It was once a tradition among the Five Civilized Tribes that a pregnant woman be banished from the group two or three days before her child was due. She was considered unclean by the others—an unwanted outcast. So she went alone to the brush and hid herself until the baby was born. This do-it-yourself plan of childbearing had been the rule during Wassie's mother's time. And there was one other part to the custom: the mother named her child for the first thing she saw after its birth. This accounts for the great abundance of Foxes, Redbirds, Deers, and Blue Eagles in the Oklahoma telephone directories. Obviously, Wassie's mother had seen a guinea hen as she started out of the woods with her baby.

Wassie was the hands-down winner of the title of Ugliest Woman in the World. She had shoulders like a wrestler's, hips like a revolving crane's, and breath that reeked of the cheaper brands of canned heat. By any norm, Wassie was a problem. However, she had one redeeming trait in our eyes—a fanatical adoration of Papa.

"That Wassie Guineahen scares me," I said to Papa one day. "Every time she stumbles into the store she drives away customers. She never buys much. Why don't you tell her to stay away?"

"I couldn't do that, Sonny. Wassie's not a bad person. That stuff she drinks now makes her a little wild, but she can't afford as much whisky as she needs to get her goin'."

"A *little* wild? What about the time she knocked all the canned goods off the shelves of the Farmer's Exchange because Gus Taylor wouldn't dance with her? And she almost killed that lawyer she pinned against the Clayton Building last year! She kept bouncing his head against the bricks until the police made her stop. What was that lawyer's name?"

"I forget," Papa lied. Then he said, "Maybe Wassie had her reasons, Son. When she was the richest Indian in Creek County she had lots of friends. She was just like a generous-hearted kid the way she gave her money away! As for that lawyer, maybe she had a right to hurt him. The lawyers got fat off Wassie. She was married five times and they say that every time she got a divorce her lawyer retired! I knew her mother—Jessica. She made me promise her before she died that I'd kinda watch out for Wassie and Wassie was standin' right there when I promised. She hasn't many white friends left. I feel kinda sorry for her. Wassie's not really dangerous. Why, she wouldn't hurt a fly."

Nevertheless, I still considered Wassie a menace and ran

out of sight whenever I saw her weaving and snorting down Main Street aiming in the general direction of Papa's store.

I was in school when Wassie attacked Papa, but Mama witnessed the whole onslaught and loved to tell the story to anyone who would listen. She became very good at it. She sounded like the narrator in a Greek tragedy, pulling out all the stops for maximum effects. When Mama went to Taro to visit her people, Uncle Ed would insist that she describe what he called "the Battle of Guineahen Ridge."

"There wasn't any ridge to it," Mama corrected. "It took place in the shoe department. Wassie came in drunker than usual, and she insisted that Max let her sleep on one of the cots downstairs. He told her that there were two men Indians already on the cots and it wouldn't look right to let a woman sleep alongside them. This only made her madder. She cussed him out in Creek, Choctaw, Osage, and English. Max just patted her shoulder and told her to stretch out in one of the shoe department chairs and go to sleep there. Wassie actually sat down for a minute, but when she discovered that sitting wasn't as good as stretching she tore out of that chair like a shot out of a cannon. Max had started walking toward the front of the store. He was thinking about something else when Wassie leaped at him from behind, tackled him around the mid-section, and lunged with him to the floor.

"There was Max," Mama continued, "kicking and grunting and yelling at the top of his lungs as he crawled to his knees. And there was Wassie out cold. The sudden jolt had knocked all the wind out of her and she'd passed out.

"Max stood up, felt himself all over to see if anything was broken. He wasn't hurt at all except for a skinned place here and there and a bunch of splinters in his pants where he'd skidded on the floor. His pride was more injured than anything else. He looked at Wassie. 'Is she dead?' he asked softly. Wassie answered his question. She let out a loud belch and rolled over on her side and started snoring.

"Max stepped over Wassie and came over to where I was standing. He was shaking all over. I'll never forget how he looked at me. He looked the same way he did when he proposed! 'Annie,' he said, 'I feel like a man who's back from the dead! I sure thought I was a goner when she hit. . . . But I'm all right now, thank God!' Then he said 'Whew!' a few times until he stopped trembling. Then he pointed at Wassie on the floor and said to me, 'Annie, in my whole lifetime that there's the only man that ever knocked me off my feet—and he's a *woman!*' "

It was a glory walking down Main Street with Papa. He was king, general, conquering hero, vote getter, super-salesman, father confessor, and Trumpeter of the Morn. Whether he was walking to the post office for the morning mail, walking to the bank to talk about a check of his that had bounced, walking to the Farmer's Exchange for a midmorning snack of raw carrots and new peas, or walking to the courthouse jail to bail out Ernie Cooper, you had the feeling that the walk itself was as important to Papa as the errand to be done at the end of it.

What did he *say?*

He said, "Good *mornin'*, Mrs. Springer! Your hair is pure gold in the mornin' sun!" Mrs. Springer flipped with happiness. He said, "Get out of that car and use your legs, Harold Lane! Who wants to drive on a day like this?" He'd spy ancient Mrs. Anderson, a fragile, pink-and-white old lady whose husband, a driller of wildcat wells, had killed himself after a siege of dry holes. He'd make a sweeping bow from the waist, courtier-fashion, and croon, "Ah, Mrs. Anderson, it's the kind of day that makes a person want to live forever . . . and I hope you do!" He'd shout to friends in cars. He'd bugle at people in stores. He'd wave. He'd point. People looked for him, even when they were unaware that they were looking. Whenever he went away on a buying trip for the store, Main Street drooped.

Papa's return from New York or Chicago or St. Louis was an important occasion. He let the whole town know how glad he was to be home. "Hi, Billy! Got in on the Frisco this morning. Charley Porter sends his best regards. Bill Random's still engineerin' it. . . . Joe!" he'd holler, ducking down to shout at Joe Brand in his barbershop below sidewalk level. "Stay away from New York City, Joe. Nobody smiles there. Don't know what's eatin' 'em. One old gal acted like I was tryin' to rape her because I said, 'Good mornin', miss.' Yes, sirree! Reported me to a cop. Told him I tried to get fresh. When the cop started askin' me questions I just pointed to her bowed legs and he had to laugh. Made me mad! . . . Come by the store today, Joe. Got a special buy on some shirts in New York. . . ."

Papa bought clothes for his store the way he ate, laughed, and sweated—copiously. He was a push-over for a "special buy." When a change of style caught the manufacturers with too much of the wrong kind of merchandise on their racks, they'd pray for Max Meyer to walk in and eliminate their surplus in one fell swoop.

Papa bought 750 peg-top-trousered suits from a jobber in New York three years after peg tops were a drug on the market. Indian chiefs, teen-aged farm boys, old-age pensioners, and men who just plain didn't give a damn how they looked bought Max Meyer's peg-top suit bargains until the last one was sold. When wide-brimmed hats were the rage, count on Papa to return from Chicago loaded with fifty dozen narrow brims. When the coat with plain back came into style, Papa looked at the huge stock of belted backs packed on a New York wholesaler's racks and said, "What'll you lump off the whole lot for? Give me a bargain and I'll take 'em all. We ain't so particular about how our rear ends look down in Oklahoma!" He got them all. Miraculously, he sold them all.

His greatest challenge as a merchant was a purchase of six thousand collarless shirts. He located a wholesaler who had five hundred cases of these shirts gathering dust in a warehouse.

"Everybody wants collars attached," the wholesaler said, never dreaming that he was talking to a man who knew better. "The material is wonderful. But nobody wants a shirt without a collar."

"Let me see 'em," Papa demanded.

The shirts were made from a silk-textured material which was quite beautiful.

"The material will wear like iron," the wholesaler said. "But nobody—"

"Shut up," Papa said. "I'm superstitious. Don't keep sayin' that nobody wants a good shirt just because it don't have a collar. Take a deep breath and quote me a rock-bottom price. If it's low enough, I'll take 'em all off your hands."

The wholesaler must have inhaled from his toes. Papa bought them all.

All six thousand of the shirts were the same color—a light, muddy pongee-yellow. There wasn't a collar in the carload. Papa made a mental note that he must find in New York City a jobber who was stuck with collars. Lots of collars.

Papa was wearing one of his collarless shirts when he stepped off the Frisco. He took Mama in his arms and kissed her hungrily in front of everybody at the depot. Then he kissed each of his four children (on the mouth, always). Then he pointed to his shirt and said, "I stole it, Annie. I stole five hundred dozen of 'em. Stole 'em for thirty-five cents per."

"Are they all . . . that . . . *color?*" Mama asked cautiously.

"Isn't it beautiful? Yellow goes with everything. This material will wear like iron."

"Wonder why the collar's a different color?" Mama asked timidly. "Did you make a mistake when you put it on?"

"The collar's not supposed to match. The collar's *separate*."

"See you soon, Max!" somebody yelled from the vestibule of the club car. It was the conductor leaning out of the train, addressing Papa. As Papa waved at him, he said to Mama, "See Charley there? The conductor? He's got a *white* collar on his!"

"You mean . . . *he's* wearing one of your thirty-five-cent shirts?"

"Shhhhhh," Papa shushed. "So's the porter. See?"

Sure enough, the porter had on one of Papa's pongee shirts with a *blue* collar under his white coat.

"It would've cost me more than I paid for the shirt for a tip . . . and look how happy he is. I've never had such service in my life. You'd think I owned the Frisco!"

Papa spotted the engineer leaning out of the locomotive cab window. He, too, was wearing a pongee shirt—with no collar at all. Only a narrow white neckband and a black shirt stud underlined his Adam's apple.

"Bye, Bill! Hope I ride with you again next time I go to market."

"Thanks for the shirt, Max! I'll be in your store Saturday. Save me a box full. I like 'em!"

"See?" Papa said triumphantly. "They'll buy 'em! Feel the quality of the material, Annie." He ripped off his coat and pulled out his shirttail for Mama to examine it. "It'll wear like iron."

"Papa!" Bea said with teen-age indignation. "Put your shirt back on. People are looking at you."

"Let 'em look, sweetheart. I've got six thousand of these shirts to sell and people might as well start seein' 'em."

"I never heard of a green collar on a yellow shirt," Pearl said.

"I *like* green," Papa roared. "Who says a collar has to *match?* I bought twelve thousand collars—two for every shirt—at two cents a throw. Some are green and some are blue and seven hundred and seventy-five are white. Feel the material, Pearl. It's a five-dollar shirt. I'll sell it for a dollar and a half and throw in two collars. They'll beg for more."

Manny, who was five years old, started to whimper. "It doesn't match. Papa's shirt doesn't match his collar."

Papa wheeled around, his face crimson, his shirttail flapping in the breeze. "Shut up, you kids! Shut up *right now!* You're puttin' the *whammy* on my shirts! You're *jonah-ing* them! How'll I sell six thousand shirts if my OWN CHILDREN put a jinx on 'em?"

Mama knew the storm warnings. She quickly bent over and whispered a bribe in Manny's ear. It must have been a generous one, because Manny started blinking away his tears and saying, "Your shirt's awful pretty, Papa."

"Now *that's* the way I like to hear you talk," Papa said, pulling in his stomach and sticking the shirttail into his trousers without unbuckling his belt. "I bought these shirts at a fraction of their worth, and I'm going to sell every last one of 'em at a profit."

He did, too. It took him years to do it, but he sold them all. He sold them to dudes, to farmers, to men who wore them without collars for summertime coolness, to young men living in rooming houses who solved their laundry problem by buying five collars per shirt and wearing a different collar with the same shirt Monday through Friday. He sold them to Mrs. Adams, the seamstress, who bought three dozen and remade them into women's blouses. He sold them to old men who were homesick for collarless shirts and were happy to find them again at any price.

Dale Carnegie, Elmer Wheeler, Frank Bettger, and other supersalesmen of our era could have taken a lesson or two in selling from Papa's technique with those yellow pongee shirts.

A customer would walk in and say, "I'd like a shirt."

Papa had other shirts in stock. Shirts with collars attached. Plenty of them. He always tried to sell his "special" first. "A shirt?" he'd say absently. "Fine. *Here's* a shirt!"

"I want a shirt with a collar on it."

"*This* shirt has a collar. It has *two* collars. Feel the material. Wears like iron. Real silk pongee. Five-dollar shirt. Specially priced. Dollar and a half." (Papa called this "the Staccato Approach.")

"Show me a shirt with a collar."

"I'll *give* you two collars with this shirt." Papa would say, insistently. "Here! Take the shirt and the two collars for a dollar thirty-five."

"I—the color isn't what—"

"Feel the material. Go on. Feel it! Yellow goes with everything."

"But—"

"Mister, you can't *buy* shirts like this any more. I got the last six thousand in New York City. Look at the pearl buttons. You never find real pearl buttons on shirts any more. Look at the length of this shirttail. . . . Anything *else?*"

"Huh?"

"I said . . . anything *else?* How about a necktie? Socks? Handkerchiefs?"

"Uh . . . no. Nothing else. Just the shirt."

Then, like a bullfighter offering the bull a moment's grace before the final thrust, Papa said softly, "Two for two-fifty if you say the word."

"Oh . . . all right. Wrap them up."

You couldn't win every time. Sometimes a customer would stubbornly insist on a shirt with collar attached. Papa would pull out an Arrow or Manhattan and plunk it onto the counter in silence. Later, as he'd count the change, he'd say, "You'll never know what you passed up, sir. Outwear the one you bought two to one."

Papa was right about the material. It did wear like iron. You'd spot those silk pongee shirts all over Sapulpa for years. As I grew up I recognized them even after they'd become bandanas, scarfs, diapers, dustcloths, and sashes. You could never mistake that yellow shade. It always looked a little muddy, even after years of washings.

As a salesman, Papa was absolutely unique. It was impossible to resist him. He stultified your power to refuse. You bought from Papa when you thought you weren't buying. You bought what you didn't want. You bought what you hated. You bought what Papa thought you *ought* to buy.

His was a peculiar system of salesmanship. It combined the Socratic question-and-answer method with the razzle-dazzle of the Split T. He clinched the sale while the customer was in a state of dazed confusion.

I have watched Papa operate thousands of times. I know his system. He can still sell me anything.

When a customer would walk into his store and say innocently, "A suit. Think I'd like to see a suit," the fun would begin.

Papa wouldn't move. "So you want to buy a suit?"

"Well . . ."

"If you *really* want to buy a suit, I'll sell you one that's *right*."

Already the bargaining process had shifted to an odd and slippery plane. Leading the way to the suit department, Papa would ask, "Any special color?"

"Oh," the customer would say offhandedly, "blue, I guess."

Papa would reach for a tape measure. He'd measure the customer's shoulders, his chest, his sleeve length, his crotch, his waist, and his leg length. Then he'd reach for the suit he'd had in mind from the moment the customer entered the store.

"Try this on. No, don't *look* at it yet. Just try it on. For fit."

Before the unsuspecting victim could protest, Papa'd have the coat on him and be pushing him toward the mirror.

"It's a three-way glass. Look at the back first. No, not *that* mirror. . . . *This* is the one to look in to see the back. . . .

See how smooth the coat fits back here?" Papa would make smoothing motions on the poor fellow's back as he was saying this. "Now look at the front. . . . Here! In *this* mirror for the front. Now for the side. . . . Perfect! It's your suit, all right. It's the suit you asked for. Couldn't find anything better if we looked all day. . . . Need anything else? Shoes? Hat? A fine pongee shirt?"

"The color. Maybe the color is— Well, I think it's too dark."

There would be dead air for a full moment while Papa looked both stunned and hurt. Then he'd say, softly, patiently, "I don't think I heard you right, young man. Did you say too *dark* or too *light?*"

"Too . . . well . . . well . . . I thought . . ."

"You said blue. This suit's blue, isn't it? Have you changed your mind?"

"No . . . I—"

"You *asked* for a blue suit. This is exactly what you wanted. Could anyone ask for more? Well, *could* they?"

In a desperate effort to escape from a trap he couldn't define, the customer would hold his arms in front of him and see that the coat sleeves hit him somewhere near his elbows. "The sleeves are too short."

"Too *long* or too *short?*" Then Papa would mimic the customer. He'd stretch his arms in front of him to pull his own coat sleeves up. "Do you walk down the street like *this?* With your arms in front of you like two handle bars? Drop them to your side, naturally. Go *on! Drop* them!"

The customer would obey.

"There! Now look in the mirror. No! *Don't move your arms!* Just *look*. Sleeve length's perfect. Try on the trousers."

The customer, bruised but not yet bleeding, would venture one last feint. "The pants. They're a little too tight in the waist."

"Suck in your stomach," Papa would command. Then, as the man paled, Papa would grab the front of the trousers and pull. "Too *tight?* Look at this space! You mean too *loose*. Say it again. Say it again. Too *loose* or too *tight?*"

By this time the customer would be on the ropes. Papa would be calling the tailor to mark the trouser lengths.

"Cuff? Or no cuff? No, don't *bend* down. Just *look* down. There! Cuff? No cuff?"

"Uh . . . maybe I'd better . . . Haven't you anything else in . . . I mean, anything less . . . Oh, hell! Put on a cuff!"

And that's all there was to it!

My father worked his will on all of us with this same selling approach. He sold us what he thought we thought we wanted, instead of what we thought we thought we wanted.

If my mother walked into the back room where Papa was reading the newspaper in front of an open window in February, she'd say, "Max, it's too cold in here."

"What did you say, Annie dear?"

"I said . . . I said it's too cold in here."

"I'm practically perspirin'. Do you mean it's too *hot* or too *cold?*" He was unrebuttable.

Once, a visiting cousin watching my sister Bea attack

her second dessert said tactlessly, "That child eats too much, Max. You ought to watch her diet. She's too fat."

Bea began to cry.

Papa was shocked. All of his children were perfect. Bea wasn't fat. She was just healthy! In incredulous tones he demanded, "Too *what?* You mean too *thin*, don't you? Why, she eats nothing at all. I don't see how she keeps goin'. Look again. Too *fat* or too *thin?*"

The cousin was furious. Bea continued with her dessert.

I suspected Papa of counterattacking in this fashion even when he agreed perfectly with the person doing the complaining. It made little difference to him if someone was too tall or too short, or too young or too old, or too smart or too dumb. He abhorred criticism and this was his way of showing it. "Never criticize," he'd caution us. "People who criticize everything never do anything worth while."

"But, Papa—"

"Eat your soup."

"It's too hot."

"There you go again—criticizin'! Too *hot* or too *cold?*"

Whereupon he'd gulp down a spoonful of his soup which was hot enough to bring tears to his eyes. "See? It's not too hot for *me*. Stop findin' fault all the time. Once a child starts findin' fault he goes through life pickin' everything to pieces. Drink your soup now before it gets any colder."

"It's . . . too—"

"Too *what?*"

So you drank it, and only cried a little bit. It was easier that way.

It hurt Papa when he heard his grandson from St. Louis call Sapulpa a hick town. He had a fatherly feeling toward his home town. He didn't like to hear other people disparage it.

"Don't say 'hick town' where I can hear you, Ronnie. Call Sapulpa anything you want to call it, but not in front of me."

"Can I ask you a question, Grandpa?" Ronnie once asked earnestly. "Will you get mad if I ask you a question?"

"Nothing my own flesh and blood would ask me in a nice way could ever make me mad. Just don't needle me."

"I'm not needling you, Grandpa. I really want to know. Why did you pick Sapulpa for your home? Tulsa was only twelve miles away. If you'd settled in Tulsa we'd all be millionaires."

"Speak for yourself, boy!" Papa said. "I *am* a millionaire."

Ronnie had touched a delicate subject and decided to back away from it. Papa had peculiar ideas about money. No millionaire had more than he.

"But Tulsa's so *big*," the boy continued in a new direction.

"And Sapulpa's so small? Well, it wasn't always smaller than Tulsa. When your great-grandfather Philip Levy gave me my pick of towns in Oklahoma I chose Sapulpa because it looked like the winner of the two towns. Sapulpa was the division point and headquarters for the Frisco Railroad. Sapulpa was smack dab in the middle of the Glenn pool, the biggest oil strike in history! Why, in 1906, when Philip Levy built my store for me, Sapulpa was bigger than Tulsa."

"What happened?" Ronnie wanted to know.

"Nobody knows for sure. We built a big electric sign over the highway comin' into town. It had lights in ten colors, and it proclaimed: SAPULPA, THE OIL CITY OF THE SOUTHWEST! And while we were buildin' that sign Tulsa was buildin' a five-story luxury hotel where the oilmen could sleep in comfort and do their lease tradin' in the lobby. Sounds like a little thing, doesn't it? Well, I guess it was the little things that made the difference. The minute that hotel was built, Tulsa started passin' us. I knew in just a few years I'd put my money on the wrong horse, but how could I move to Tulsa? I owned my store; I'd built a great big house on Oak Street; I'd started buyin' land for the ranch. You might say I was stuck with Sapulpa. Anyway, I stuck with it for fifty years—and I can tell you that I went through hell with this town."

Ronnie listened as his grandfather told a story Oklahomans know too well.

"The oil began to play out. New pools opened up in other places. People left by the thousands. Then Tulsa took the Frisco terminal away from us. Tulsa got the oil companies, too. Sapulpa was a ghost town with its blocks of empty stores. It cost a lot of money to keep my store goin' during those bad times. Sometimes we'd go all day long without a customer. At the height of the boom I had fifty-six employees in my organization; during the bad time I had one man, and didn't need him. If it hadn't been for the oil royalties that kept comin' in every month, the store would've gone bankrupt.

"No town in America was harder hit than Sapulpa,

Oklahoma. I could've saved a lot of money by callin' it quits and closin' my store the way the others did, but, by golly, I wasn't gonna quit till the town came back! People began to return to the empty houses just as I knew they would. The glass factories, the brickyards, and the pottery hired workers. Business got good again. My father had always told me to tend to the lands or tend to the store— but not to try and do both. I waited till I got a good lease on my store building from the Safeway people; then I finally took my father's advice. I was forty years gettin' around to it, but forty years ain't so long when you consider how old the world is."

Ronnie sat quietly while his grandfather finished the story.

"So you see, Sapulpa's not exactly a hick town. No town's a hick town that's got the gumption to fight back like that. Thirty thousand people lived here durin' the boom. There aren't half that many here today." He paused. "And Tulsa's got a quarter of a million!" Papa sighed. "Yep, Ronnie. Your grandfather picked the wrong horse. But he sure got a ride for his money."

2. THE GOOD EARTH

Although he liked to call himself a farmer, Papa's achievements in the world of agriculture would not inspire a 4-H youngster to increased effort. He neither awakened with the sun nor did he go to bed with the chickens. If he'd had to live off what he grew he would have gone hungry. There was nothing *in*tensive about his approach to farming. He was *ex*tensive in the broadest sense of the word. His potato patch was never under two acres. He had at least an acre of string beans and an acre and a half of tomatoes. We still try to forget the year he planted five acres of Bermuda onions to the windward side of the Big House where we lived on the ranch. He couldn't dispose of the bushels he gathered, so he left the remainder of the crop to rot on the ground. People claimed that when the breeze was right they could smell those onions in Tulsa, seventeen miles away.

Papa's ranch hugged Highway 66 for almost three miles, beginning at a high point some five miles from Sapulpa and extending to the city limits of a small village called Kellyville. Here, where his domain terminated, he created a townsite of his own, the Max Meyer Addition to Kellyville, with streets named after members of his family.

So far as he knew, Papa was the only Jewish farmer in Oklahoma. He kept beating the drum for a back-to-the-soil movement for the Jews of America. Back from what he didn't say.

Word of his farming activities reached a magazine called *Judaism, USA*. The editor wrote Papa a letter asking for more information about his career as a farmer. Papa answered at great length, enclosing pictures of his silos, his white-faced bull, his chicken houses, his nursery, and one of himself and Mama on the front porch of the Big House. The published article was entitled "Jews Can Be Successful Farmers." It closed with an editorial plea for more Jews to follow Papa's lead. A close-up of Papa at the wheel of his Cadillac helped convey the idea that a successful farmer could expect to live in the lap of luxury.

Neither Papa nor the article mentioned the best crop on the ranch: a cluster of thirty-one oil wells on one 160-acre tract. It takes a lot of harvesting to beat that for success.

Bea and Pearl were embarrassed when Papa told their boy friends that he was a farmer by profession.

"A farmer!" Pearl scoffed. "Saying that is the surest way to start a prospective son-in-law running in the other direction. I don't think you *want* your daughters to get married."

"Can't you just say you're retired?" Bea suggested. "Nobody wants to marry a farmer's daughter, but the daughter of a retired man is supposed to be a catch."

Papa looked hurt, as he always did when the girls ganged up on him. "Ashamed of your poor old Daddy?" he asked plaintively.

"Of course not," Pearl replied. "But Papa, you're *not* a farmer. You don't wear overalls. You don't push a plow. You don't milk a cow. You don't know a hog from a sow."

"Ow . . . ow . . . ow . . ." Papa howled. "I'll take those accusations one at a time. I don't wear overalls because they don't manufacture 'em for men with big stomachs. I don't milk cows because I don't have to. I bought all those electric milkers so's my cows would be untouched by human hands. And as to knowin' the difference between a hog and a sow I can guarantee you that so long as this ranch is mine, it's gonna be a kosher farm—*no hogs allowed!*"

Papa's farm may have been kosher, but some of his farming techniques weren't. The nearest he ever came to making money on what he grew was during the days of the AAA when he discovered to his delight that it was profitable *not* to grow things. For years he had lost money on the crops he harvested. Now he could make money by doing nothing. He signed up for every government subsidy for which he was remotely eligible. He didn't read the fine print. He just signed. And he hit the jackpot. The green, perforated cardboard checks from the U. S. Treasury came to his post-office box by the fistful.

Papa stayed within the regulations, but he liked to talk as though he were getting away with murder. He referred to the U. S. Government as his "farmin' partner." He drove the local farm agent, Al Phillips, to the point of suicide every time he entered his office.

"Good morning, Max."

"Good mornin', Al. I came in to ask you how much my partner will pay me for not growin' rubber trees."

"Now, Max! You shouldn't make jokes like that. You know very well that this subsidy program is a lifesaver for the farmer."

"A lifesaver? Why, Al, it's better than that. It's bringin' 'em back from the dead. Take peanuts—"

Al began to squirm.

"I never raised peanuts in my life. Now I get a check every month for not raisin' peanuts. Take cotton—"

Al's face began to redden.

"You know how much I hate growin' cotton. Cotton saps the lifeblood out of the land. So ain't it nice of my farmin' partner to pay me money every month not to grow the stuff?"

"Max, you know very well that you signed up for your maximum allotment of eighty-seven acres of cotton. That's a lot of cotton."

"You *force* me to grow that much! I have to grow eighty-seven acres of cotton so's I'll get paid for *not* growin' five hundred acres. And don't start givin' me that soybean look,

Al Phillips. I never grew a soybean in my life. Hell. I never even *saw* a soybean till you signed me up. Now I've got every available inch, includin' the whole front yard, in soybeans. Soybeans are comin' out of my ears."

"Max, you know very well you applied for the full soybean program."

"I'm applyin' for *all* the programs. A man'd either be a darned fool or a Republican not to take free soybeans and plant 'em every place he can find to put 'em when he's gettin' paid by the acre for doin' it."

"Maybe you're not a born farmer, Max," Al ventured.

"I'm a born *not*-farmer!" Papa said. "I like not-farmin' better than farmin'. I'm not-raisin' hogs to please my partner. I get paid for it. My partner doesn't know that I wouldn't raise hogs on my place if he paid me double what he's payin' for the soybeans. I'm not-raisin' wheat and I'm not-raisin' rye. However, I'm *not* not-raisin' alfalfa this year because I've got to grow *something* to feed the cattle. Tell me the truth, Al. How much is it worth to you and my partner for me to not-grow rubber trees?"

Al began to get mad. His temples started to throb. "Max Meyer, you know very well you've got the largest cotton allotment in Creek County. You'll make more money from your cotton patch than you ever made off the whole ranch. You've got no right to complain."

"Who's complainin'?" Papa inquired innocently. "I just want more. We farmers haven't been gettin' anything for what we raised for years. Now you're payin' us fairly well for what we don't raise, and I for one want to co-operate to the fullest. If you won't let me not-raise rubber trees, how about lettin' me not-raise flax? I ain't particular what I'm not-raisin' just so's I get those green checks every month for not-raisin' it!"

Papa still spits whenever he sees a white-faced bull. He bought such a bull for one thousand dollars, and the herd to go with it for five thousand more. The cattle hadn't found all the shady spots in the pasture when the price of registered cattle fell to the lowest point in years. "Their faces are white, but my face is red," Papa moaned.

His ill-fated venture into the cattle business would have been even more disastrous than it was if Papa hadn't found a new fairy god-partner in the Frisco Railroad.

The Frisco cut the ranch in two, lengthwise. For almost three miles the tracks followed a steep grade through the ranch property. We used to tell the time of day and night by the passenger trains between Oklahoma City and St. Louis. At night it was a lovely sight to look east from the back porch of the Big House and see the bright-lighted Frisco weaving in and out of the trees as it climbed slowly toward Oklahoma City or sped downhill to Tulsa.

The railroad refused to fence its right of way. Papa made formal requests for a fence, to no avail. Although he pretended to be furious at the railroad's refusal to protect his cattle from their trains, he was secretly tickled pink.

One of the most frequent visitors to the ranch was Mr. Jack Fitzgerald, the claims adjuster for the Frisco. He pretended to be disgusted with Papa for encouraging his cattle to get onto the tracks, but it was plain from the size of his settlements that he genuinely liked Papa.

"Hello, Max, you old rascal," Mr. Fitzgerald would begin. "Which one of your prize animals has our trains bumped into now?"

Papa would shake hands, give him a comfortable chair by a south window, and go to fetch him a shot of bourbon whisky. Mr. Fitzgerald's standard shot was a water tumbler filled to the brim. In a few minutes they'd both be laughing, slapping their thighs, and carrying on over some private joke.

Once, I walked into the room where Mr. Fitzgerald was sitting. Papa was in the kitchen refilling Mr. Fitzgerald's glass. Mr. Fitzgerald was looking out of the window at Papa's nursery.

"Young man," he said, "your father is the best cattleman in the U.S.A. Every other rancher in the country is losing money on cattle since the bottom fell out of the market, but not Max. He's selling his herd off, one at a time, to the Frisco Railroad."

I came to Papa's defense. "If the Frisco had a *fence* . . ."

Mr. Fitzgerald roared. "If they had a fence your father'd have a fit. The Frisco could have built a fence of platinum for what we've paid Max for letting the right cows on our tracks at the wrong time."

"Pay no attention to him, Son," Papa said as he handed the drink to Mr. Fitzgerald. "So long as the Frisco won't build a fence, they're goin' to pay me what my cows are worth."

"What they're *worth?*" Mr. Fitzgerald slopped some of his whisky over the sides of the glass as he made his point. "You mean ten *times* what they're worth! I swear, Max, some day you're gonna present a claim to the Frisco for burnin' a hole in the middle of your lake!"

"It's a possibility," Papa said, making a mental note to think that over.

As the motorist speeds down Highway 66 today he may see, across the road from the Big House where Papa lives, a faded sign in front of a shambles that was once a nursery sales office. The sign reads:

MAX MEYER NURSERY AND LANDSCAPE COMPANY.
WHY PAY MORE?

When the sign was new it marked the spot of one of Papa's most ambitious soil projects: his plunge into the world of evergreen and rosebush.

Instead of beginning modestly and then expanding, Papa started his trees and shrubs business on a big scale with every intention of growing larger. He located the nursery a hundred yards south of the Big House, on a flat, rich part of the ranch which fronted the highway. Across the highway he built a nursery stand. Nearby, he built a nurseryman's home.

Papa grew little from seeds. He preferred to buy nursery stock that was already started, plant it, and then transplant it to the customer's yard.

One nursery project that Papa did nurse from infancy was a shipment of twenty-five thousand fruit-tree seedlings which everyone in the family helped to "bud." Papa said he got the whole lot "for a song" and he asked everybody we knew to help get the seedlings started.

I was ten years old at the time, but I still remember the stifling heat, the choking dirt, the cramped muscles, and the monotony of scooting along the powdery ground from seedling to seedling. The routine budding operation consisted of splitting each stem with a knife, inserting the bud into the slit, tying the bud around with a rubber band, and then proceeding to the next seedling. This is a good way to get a permanent prejudice against any kind of fruit that doesn't come in a can.

A terrible thing happened to this particular crop of fruit trees. Papa and his nurseryman had an argument and the nurseryman quit in a huff. This in itself was not unusual. Papa never saw root to root with any nurseryman he ever hired. But the unfortunate thing about this particular departure was that the nurseryman, out of sheer spite and meanness, changed the name plates on all the rows of fruit trees, systematically switching the signs that told which variety was which.

Papa, unaware of this villainy, and wholly dependent upon the signs, blithely sold whole orchards of peach trees which turned out to be cherries, plums that turned out to be pears, and apples that turned out to be pecans. This incident was one of the main reasons why Papa quit the nursery business. The repercussions lasted for years.

Papa had acres of evergreens, junipers, and ornamental shrubs. He bought them from wholesalers' catalogues. He kept all of his catalogues and nursery materials in the basement of the Big House. Here he spent hours poring over them. He was always in search of close-outs of nursery stock, just as he had sought close-outs of wearing apparel when he had the store. From collarless shirts to fruit trees, Papa was a push-over for "a bargain on the whole lot." By asking the supplier "to make me a price on all you've got," he bought ten thousand cypresses, five thousand spruces, and twelve thousand cherry laurels. He figured he had room a-plenty, and he could always muster up a small army of diggers from his WPA Row colony of indigent tenants whom he fed, clothed, and fathered. The rows weren't always straight, but the stock got planted.

It was illuminating to watch Papa conducting would-be buyers between these nursery rows, answering all of their questions without the slightest hesitation. He figured that if he gave the impression of knowing all the answers the customers would be satisfied. Within an hour's selling time he called the same juniper a Blue Arizona, a Blue Pfitzer, a Blue Haven, and a Blue Silver Glauca. He was vague about the heredity but positive about the color. It was blue.

Papa's sales approach for the nursery was definitely on the soft side. Madison Avenue specialists would probably refer to it as the "only God can make a tree" approach. He had no price list, adjusting the price to fit the customer.

I remember once when a prospect pointed to a dogwood tree and asked, "How much?"

Papa paused, looked perplexed, and replied, "Well, how much *should* it cost? Ten cents? A million dollars? Price is relative. Who can put a price tag on a beautiful flowerin' dogwood tree—one of God's finest creations?"

This answer rocked the buyer back on his heels. He groped for words and began defensively, "Well, what I meant was . . ."

"I know," Papa replied vaguely. And then, magnanimously, he added, "I can tell that you want that dogwood tree. You love it. You're afraid you can't afford it. Well, I want you to have it. Go on, take it for two dollars."

"That's not enough. You—"

"Won't hear any more!" Papa said, calling for one of his men to come and dig up the dogwood tree which he was giving away in this spirit of *noblesse oblige*.

Papa was right. Price was relative. Besides, he had two thousand more dogwood trees exactly like this one. He had bought and planted them two years earlier. He'd got them on a close-out at two cents apiece.

In the springtime the unsold, transplanted flowering shrubs bloomed as gaily in their nursery rows as their sold sisters bloomed in the yards of customers. Masses and masses of forsythias, weigelas, and spiraeas created a yellow-pink-and-white fairyland which caused more than one cross-country tourist to slow down and marvel as he passed the ranch.

Despite summer drought and heat, Papa's roses bloomed both profligately and prolifically. He would buy thousands of rosebushes from wholesale nurseries near Tyler, Texas, every spring and keep them dormant in sand beds. Then he'd cut out exquisitely colored pictures from nursery magazines and advertisements and paste these tempters on cardboard posters for the various kinds of rosebushes. The live picture sold the dormant bush. His paper rose garden was a work of art.

On weekends there would be as many as twenty-five or thirty cars at a time parked around the nursery stand, buying rosebushes at bargain prices. Papa hired my brother and me and some of our friends to help do the selling. It was an easy job. We took the roses out of their beds when the customer pointed to the variety he wished. Then we wrapped old newspapers around the bushes while the customer paid the cashier (one of my sisters). By the time I was twelve years old I had learned to distinguish one kind of rosebush from another without having to consult the poster or name tag. With a little experience, anyone can tell a dormant Mrs. Herbert Hoover from a dormant Pink Columbia, or a Kaiserin Wilhelmina from an American Beauty.

Papa said that all of the leftover bushes belonged to Mama, who loved roses. Surely no rose-lover ever received so many from a single admirer. Papa planted all the unsold rosebushes along the highway, hundreds and hundreds of them, and they bloomed all summer long. All it took was a basket, some snippers, and a half-hour to go "rose picking." Every container in the house was filled with roses all summer. There was half an acre of white roses, almost an acre of pink ones, and row after row of yellows and reds. Of all the crops that Papa ever planted, his crop of roses is the one I'll remember the longest.

Papa's greatest challenge turned out to be Chinese elms. "Ellums" he called them. He bought one hundred thousand tiny Chinese elm trees in one lot. The largest ones were no more than six inches tall. This was far and away his most ambitious nursery project. For weeks Papa's helpers planted the elms in long rows adjoining the flowering shrubs, in clusters along the side of the hill near the nurseryman's house, and helter-skelter along the Frisco right of way east of the nursery proper. Multitudes remained. Papa didn't have the heart to let them go unplanted, so he cleared a large area south of the house, behind the rose patch. He planted these leftover elms close together in rows a half mile long. There were eight of them, just a few feet apart.

The Chinese elm is a hardy, fast-growing tree that fills the need for shade in a hurry. "You won't have to wait a lifetime to have your trees," Papa would tell new home-owners whose yards were barren of any kind of tree or shrub. As time passed and the trees grew rapidly, it was a major job digging up the large elms, balling them, wrapping them with burlap, and transplanting them. Most of the Chinese elms in the nursery itself were sold, but the eight long rows of leftovers were never touched. These trees grew taller and taller. Their branches interlocked. Their trunks almost touched each other in the crowded quarters.

If you drop in on Papa today and take one of his guided tours through his Big House, with its many rooms, you'll look out of the upstairs' bedroom window at the panorama of farm land, turn away, and then wheel around again to take a longer look. Papa will be saying, "Over there's where the nursery used to be. Help became too much of a problem." Then Papa will point to the phenomenon which is making you blink: a long, thin, rectangular expanse of big trees in uniform rows stretching into the distance. The absence of trees on all sides of this wooded area accentuates the incongruity.

"Those are Chinese ellums," he'll explain. "They got too big to sell. If you'd like one for your home it can be arranged. No charge. My crew will dig it up and ball it for you. All *you* have to do is worry about the transportation."

You'll continue to stare at the army of trees, standing like a division of soldiers at close-order attention. You'll say what everyone says, "It's—it's a regular forest!"

"Yep," Papa will agree. "Twenty years ago I planted some tiny saplings, and now I've got a whole forest of Chinese ellums growin' alongside my house! They certainly don't do any *harm* standin' out there. When the wind blows from the right direction it makes a real musical sound through their leaves."

You're still staring at the overpopulated Chinese elms as Papa takes your arm to continue the tour, murmuring reassuringly, "I've got all the firewood I'm gonna need for the next hundred years."

Every man, at one time in his life, gets a wild hair to raise chickens. Papa's urge to go into the chicken business took place so many years ago that we children have only the fuzziest memories of numberless baby chicks cheeping and chirping in nervous confusion around the lime-sprinkled chicken yard, of rows of incubators hatching new batches, and of crates of grown chickens being carted away on pickup trucks.

There haven't been chickens in quantity on the ranch for years, but the vast chicken plant remains—the brooder house, the nesting building, the pens—all of them in a huge, dilapidated compound behind the caretaker's house on the way down to the lake.

Only Papa can tell the story of what happened when he invested in chickens. It may be too good a story to be factually accurate. I don't know for sure. Every time I hear Papa tell it with gusto I'm convinced that it's true.

"The chicken business? Oh, my goodness, Sonny boy, don't *ever* go into the chicken business! I spent a small fortune buildin' a chicken layout. I'd been better off if I paid a dollar apiece for eggs and ten dollars apiece for the fryers your mother cooked on Sunday."

Papa's eyes wrinkled up in a smile as he warmed to his story.

"Oh, on paper you'll make a mint from raisin' chickens. They cost next to nothing when they're tiny, they grow up fast, and then you sell them for a good price. Simple? Hah! It doesn't work out that way. *One* gets sick and they *all* get sick. Every time it rains they have the opportunity to drown themselves. You gotta watch hawks and dogs and chicken thieves and—"

When he said the word "thieves" Papa sped on in another direction.

"Sonny, there are several varieties of chicken thieves. Not all of 'em operate after dark. In fact, you actually *pay* some of 'em to steal chickens from you. Take the feller who answered my ad for a chicken man. He spoke real nice and seemed to know his chickens. I gave him the caretaker's house to live in, and I made a deal with him whereby half of all the chickens we raised belonged to him for takin' care of 'em.

"I left him completely alone. When he wanted more baby chicks, he just went to the hatchery and bought 'em and charged 'em to me. Charged the feed, too, and all the medical supplies. If you think people need a lot of medicine, you oughta get to know chickens! Chickens are *always* sick!

"This man was supposed to keep track of what he sold, but I never saw his figures. He was pleasant to talk to, but he never wanted to talk finances.

"Finally I called on him and said I thought we oughta have some sorta reckonin'. He got a real sad expression on his face. He sighed, took off his straw hat, and said, 'Why, Mr. Meyer, I thought you *knew*.'

" 'Knew *what?*' I asked.

" 'Knew that all of our chickens got sick,' he said.

" 'Even so,' I said, 'there are still a heck of a lot of 'em runnin' around the chicken yard there. You've been sellin' 'em by the crateful for days.'

"Believe it or not, Sonny, that feller stood there calmly, looked me in the eye, and said, 'Them that you're talkin' about are *my* half, Mr. Meyer. Y'see, *your* half died.' And I couldn't prove they hadn't!"

3. A MEDIUM OF EXCHANGE

Money isn't everything. I know. Papa
told all of his children three times a
day: money isn't everything.

So thoroughly did Papa convince me that money doesn't
bring happiness that I'm still amazed when I discover
somebody who is rich and who appears to be contented.
Rich people should be sad. Because they have too much
money. By the same token, poor people should be happy.
Because money isn't everything.

I remember some squatters on our ranch during the
Depression. They threw together some shacks from old
lumber, corrugated iron, and rusted old tanks and lived
at the foot of the hill near the bend of the highway, about
a mile from the Big House. People kept advising Papa to
make them move away, but he didn't have the heart to
do it. "They'll go when times get better," he said.

Every time we'd pass the squatters' shacks, Papa would

58

take one hand off the steering wheel and point in their direction. "Just look at those people," he'd say. "They haven't a worry in the world. They're broke, but happy. A lot happier than most people who are rich."

Whenever my father would prove his point, my sister Pearl would study the unshaved men in patched overalls, the faded women, and the frail children. Long after the car had passed the squatters, Pearl would turn around and stare at them through the rear window.

One day we were driving toward the ranch listening to Papa's "money isn't everything" lecture. He concluded, as usual, by pointing at the squatters and saying, "Look at those people. Happy as larks."

Pearl, who was usually quiet and reticent, spoke up from the back seat in a soft voice. "They don't look happy to me," she said. "They look awful."

Mama nudged her quickly, and frowned her quiet.

"Money isn't everything," Papa said brightly. "Just because people don't dress fancy doesn't mean they aren't happy. Those folks haven't a care in the world. No money. No troubles!"

This time Pearl didn't look back.

After I was grown I would try to lecture Papa (in a nice way) about spending money. He'd look at me pityingly and say, "Sonny boy, you take money too seriously. Money isn't worth worryin' over. Never forget that money is only a medium of exchange."

Despite Papa's sincere advice I continued to worry about money, and I still do. I will continue to worry about it so long as it's my job to see that there's enough in the bank to cover his expenditures. Show me an unworried Prime Minister and I'll show you a jaundiced Chancellor of the Exchequer.

I worried mostly when both ends wouldn't meet. Papa, who never worried, had an uncanny way of bringing the ends together. When all seemed lost he'd sell a lease to a drilling company or find a buyer for some forgotten city lots or sell a hillside of his "natural stone." For a whole day the ends would meet. Then Papa would get one of his wild spending hairs and pull them apart again.

Leo Burt, the long-suffering cashier of the Sapulpa National Bank, called me one day to tell me that Papa was overdrawn—again. "Keep your shirt on," I told him. "Money isn't worth worrying over. It's only a medium of exchange." This went over with him like a ton of bricks. He couldn't understand such a philosophy and he said as much. The supply always had to balance the demand, he thought. This "banker's philosophy" bored Papa. Life is exciting, he insisted, only when the supply can't catch up to the demand or vice versa. "Secretly, Leo Burt envies me," Papa told me once. "He wants to be daring and he can't be because he's a banker. Money is to have fun with and he never has any fun."

Most of the time Papa was overdrawn just a few dollars. Occasionally a few hundred. Once, Leo Burt shouted at me on the telephone, "Your father! He's three thousand seven hundred and thirty-six dollars and twenty-seven cents overdrawn—and don't hand me that stuff about money not being worth worrying over. *This* much money *is!*" I dropped everything and went to the bank.

Most of the time I covered Papa's overdrafts without remonstrating with him. His maddening reply—"Don't get so excited, Sonny boy. It's only money!"—did something to my nerve endings. It made me jumpy.

Despite his ephemeral balances, Papa was one of the bank's best customers from a check-writing standpoint. He never wrote less than three hundred checks a month. Most of them were under a dollar. Papa paid his workers by the hour and often on the hour. Sometimes he paid by the half-hour. The Indian boys, who lived permanently and worked sporadically at the ranch, Ernie Cooper, Papa's stonemason and constant companion, and other retainers received from two to five checks per day for their work, in amounts ranging from seventy-five cents to a dollar and a half. Papa never did know the Indians' real names. He made their checks payable to "Big Indian" and "Little Indian." They endorsed the checks that way and the bank honored them. Ernie Cooper's checks were made payable simply to "Ernie" or "Ern." At least fifty checks each month were made out to "Gus." Gus was Gus Taylor, who owned the Farmer's Exchange. Gus served as Papa's money-changer, telephone message taker, and free-lunch supplier.

Once in a while one of Papa's eternally hot checks would bounce, with the message "insufficient funds." Either Leo Burt would forget to call or someone else in the bank would process it. Papa would storm into the bank, corner Leo, and demand indignantly, "What's the big idea? You make more money on my bank service charge every month than you make off the glass factory. Tell whoever is new back in the bookkeepin' department not to make a mistake like this again." If Leo would try to protest, Papa would start shaking his hand and smiling, "No hard feelings. We all make mistakes. Just tell your bookkeeper not to let it happen a second time!" and he'd be out the front door.

Nobody ever tried to forge Papa's signature on a check. It was unforgeable. Papa signed his checks with two wild flourishes, one for "Max," the other for "Meyer." Neither flourish was legible. One school of thought believed that Papa signed his checks in Hebrew. Others insisted that he just scratched with a pen a certain way. The thing that puzzled me was the way it always looked the same.

Eventually Papa put the bank account in my name. When he wanted money he'd come to me and I'd write the check for what he needed. Now Leo Burt could begin his tirades with "*You*—" instead of "Your *father*—"

I succeeded in consolidating some of the salary checks to Big Indian and Little Indian. I also encouraged Papa to charge items like groceries at the Farmer's Exchange, gasoline from his tenant's filling station, and ice cream at the Corner Drug.

Now I knew approximately how much money was available when Papa got the spending urge. If I could meet his request by getting rentals in advance or kiting a check until the oil payment arrived, I'd do it. Otherwise I'd have to ask him to wait.

"Wait?" Papa would say, hurt that his own son who had the power to write all checks should refuse old Dad the price of twelve wagon wheels for decorations along the highway. After all, it was only money. One shouldn't deny one's own father such a small thing as money.

Whenever Papa walked into my office humming to himself, I knew what he wanted and automatically reached for the checkbook. "Sonny boy, give me five dollars. I need some groceries and I have to pay to get a flat fixed."

"You don't have to tell me what you spend your money for, Papa. When the money's in the bank it's yours to spend for whatever you want. Better let me write the check out for ten."

"No! Five's plenty. When I need more I'll come for it." And he did.

"Sonny Boy," he'd begin, "I need fifty dollars. . . ." Or five hundred dollars. Or five thousand dollars. The amount was irrelevant. The need was all that mattered. Papa had no special approach for large sums. The only clue I had that a big bite was coming was the humming. He hummed louder when he needed more.

What a lovely way to live! So few can afford it! I know many millionaires who envy Papa his contempt for money. I rejoice that he had a financial flunky to do his money worrying for him, even if that flunky had to be me. Many and many a time he'd sit down in the armchair across from my desk, stretch out his legs, and expostulate on the subject of money. "It's a good thing I'm not a spendthrift, Sonny boy. Your Dad doesn't spend money on liquor or cigarettes or clothes or [self-consciously] women. I only buy necessities." This was true. Papa's necessities ranged from food to gasoline to silos to lakes to flagpoles, and included all land which adjoined his own on all sides.

Despite his conservative politics, Papa came dangerously close to socialism in his attitude toward money. Money within the family was interchangeable. What was his belonged equally to one (or all) of his children. By the same token, what belonged to one (or all) of his children should be shared in common with whoever needed it. It upset Papa when one of his children would say proprietarily, "That's mine!" When he'd hear it, Papa would roar, "That's *whose?* What's one's is the other's around this house, and *that's the way it's goin' to be!*" Papa would give the shirt off his back to one of his own (and he did, unto fifth cousins). If, on the other hand, Papa ever needed a shirt he fully expected someone to strip for him.

Papa inherited this "what's mine is yours and what's yours is mine" feeling from his mother. Grandma Meyer spent her entire lifetime "doing for others" with manipulated funds. Grandma was a woman of action. She didn't believe in wasted motion. I learned this the hard way.

I was visiting my cousins in Hot Springs, Arkansas, and went fishing on the lake with them while the famous Hot Springs Fishing Derby was going on. No one was more surprised than I when a nine-pound bass chose my hook for immortality. I brought the fish to Grandma's house, parked it on the kitchen sink, and ran upstairs to change my clothes before taking it to the Chamber of Commerce for my prize.

Grandma wandered into the kitchen, took a look at the fish, saw her work cut out for her, and took over. In her direct, straight-to-the-point way she associated fish with food and food with cooking. When I walked into the kitchen a moment too late I saw my beautiful bass— beheaded, betailed, and boiling in a pot studded with carrots and celery.

"*Your* fish!" Grandma said. "Shame on you! Around here everything belongs to everybody. In a family one must share."

Grandma Meyer was a fund raiser the same way that she was a fish snatcher. She was always in need of money to send to her friends and relatives in the old country. The old country was mostly Poland. Sometimes the old country included Austria, Hungary, and parts of Russia.

Grandma Meyer had her own UNICEF organization a full two generations before the United Nations ever existed. She was constantly sending money, clothing, food, and boat tickets to relatives, friends, friends of relatives, and relatives of friends in the old country. From her modest house in Hot Springs, Arkansas, she pulled wires, cut tape, and worked miracles. She told me once that she herself was responsible for at least five hundred former residents of the old country now being citizens of the United States. These newcomers to our shores were as prolific as they were enthusiastic. They became parents, grandparents, and great-grandparents to thousands of new Americans.

Grandma Meyer, who brought this about, was one of the unsung heroines of the free world.

Grandma Meyer would have depopulated the old country had she had the money for transportation and the signatures for affidavits of support. Her share-the-wealth ideas brought her to Sapulpa for a visit when oil was discovered in the Max Meyer Addition to Kellyville. No sooner had she kissed Mama on both cheeks and put the gefilte fish she had brought into the icebox than she told Mama the reason for her journey. She wanted some of the oil money to send to the old country so the people there could come here. She made it very plain that this new money belonged to all the blood relations even though an ocean had kept them from being introduced up to now. She asked Mama point-blank if Mama had any objections. Mama said that whatever Papa did with the money was all right with her. Grandma kissed her on both cheeks and got ready for her interview with Papa. She knew she couldn't lose.

Grandma Meyer did her selling job in Yiddish so we children never did get the whole gist of her arguments, but it was apparent that she reminded her son that money wasn't everything and that the more you give, the more you get. She cried a great deal as she read Papa letters from her sisters (who wouldn't themselves leave Poland but who seemed eager to send the rest of their countrymen to Arkansas). The letters must have been very sad because Papa screwed up his face to keep from crying and kept blowing his nose.

Then Grandma laid her cards on the table. She showed him her own quotas and waiting lists. "I want, Max, that you should give me from each oil well the first one thousand dollars."

Even to one who had been carefully indoctrinated in the theory that money wasn't everything this request came as something of a surprise.

Before Papa could answer, Grandma asked, "How many wells will there be?"

"I don't know, Mama," Papa said truthfully. "Maybe two . . . maybe four . . . with luck, six."

"You'll never miss the money, Max. You'll be blessed for it a million times. Give me your promise."

"I promise to send you money, Mama."

"Not just money. The first thousand dollars from each new well. Tell me you'll do this thing and my mind can rest easy."

"I'll think it over, Mama."

"Decide right now," Grandma insisted. "I brought some gefilte fish with me and I'd like to serve it to you right now with peace of mind."

Grandma didn't believe in wasted motion. And Papa adored gefilte fish.

There were thirty-one wells. Grandma Meyer got thirty-one thousand dollars. She became Big Business. Not a cent did she keep for herself. She expected no repayment from the dozens of transplantees, and was not disappointed when they forgot to write after settling down in New York, Chicago, Kansas City, and Little Rock. She couldn't worry

about those who had used the communal money to come
to the land of opportunity. She kept adding names to her
lists and praying for more oil.

Papa felt the same way about cars that he felt about
money. They were necessary, but they weren't worth
worrying over. If money was merely a medium of exchange,
a car was merely a medium of transportation. It took you
where you wanted to go, with no back talk. If the road
was good, fine. If the road was rough or unused, so what?
If there was no road at all, he made his own road.

The book on Papa and cars hasn't been written. Its
chapters would be entitled "Papa and the Stutz," "Papa
and the Winton," "Papa and the Marmon," "Papa and
the Jordan," "Papa and the Pierce-Arrow," "Papa and
the Cadillac." Papa preferred heavy cars. "I feel safer in
them," he said. His 1958 license bill included a '48 Packard
sedan, a '45 Dodge coupe, a '41 Lincoln Continental, a
'50 Chevrolet pickup, two tractors of unknown vintage,
and a '58 Buick. The Buick was a replacement for a '54
Chrysler Imperial which Papa would still be driving except
for a semantics slip. Papa told Little Indian to "drain all the
oil out of the car." Then Papa refilled the car with oil
which he had bought wholesale. Little Indian took Papa
literally. "All the oil" included the oil in the transmission,
too. This hadn't occurred to Papa until the terrible smoking
and clanging and jerking started. By then it was too late.
The transmission was shot.

Papa asked for a consultation. "It's silly to pay four
hundred dollars for a repair bill," he argued, "when I can

trade this Chrysler in on a fifty-eight Buick which is bein'
sacrificed because the fifty-nines are almost here. What
do you think, Sonny boy?"

"I don't know," I replied truthfully. "But whatever you
decide, get rid of the Chrysler. Let's not have another
retainer on the license rolls."

The Buick people didn't want the Chrysler, but Papa
talked them into sending a wrecker to tow it in and allowing
him three hundred dollars on the trade-in.

Papa needed a full-time master mechanic on his payroll.
His garage bills were prodigious. Everything happened to
Papa's cars. He fractured axles. He amputated fenders. He
battered brakes. He gummed up gears. He burned bearings.
He ruined radiators. He tortured timing.

Papa had tire trouble the way some people have foot
trouble. Nothing helped. New tires, secondhand tires, re-
caps—all went flat as soon as they got on his cars. He just
didn't vibrate to tires.

Papa was philosophical about flats. You had 'em. You
fixed 'em. People usually stopped to help him. Everybody
knew Max and you couldn't pass him by when he was
sweating over a rim on a hot day. More than one person
accused Papa of enjoying flats because they gave him a
chance to visit with people he hadn't seen in years.

Twenty years ago Papa took Bea and Pearl on an overland trip to New York in a new seven-passenger Cadillac
he had bought for the trip. The purpose of the expedition
was to get Bea's mind off Harold Miller, the young St.
Louis lawyer who had asked Papa formally for Bea's hand
in marriage and been refused (formally) three times. The

trip was a failure from the start, because Bea decided for herself she wouldn't be separated from Harold any longer and made up her mind to marry him when she returned to college.

I still remember answering the telephone and hearing the operator say, "We have a collect call from Max Meyer in Marietta, Ohio."

"O.K.," I said, wondering why Papa would be calling from there.

"Hello, Sonny," Papa said loudly. "Let me talk to your mother."

I got Mama and heard Papa yelling at her from Ohio, "Don't worry, Annie. We're all safe. Nobody is hurt."

"What happened?" Mama asked.

"I must have dozed off and we hit another car," Papa yelled. "But nobody's hurt, thank goodness."

"My God!" Mama said, with feeling.

"Wire me forty-five hundred dollars, Annie. They're orderin' a new Cadillac from Detroit for me and it'll be here tomorrow."

"My God!" Mama said, with more feeling.

She got the money at the bank the next morning, and Papa and the girls drove home in the new car.

During the seven-passenger-Cadillac days Papa proved his theory about money. It was not worth worrying about. All it was made for was to spend. And he spent it. For three years the oil royalties from the Kellyville lease amounted to a thousand dollars a day. This was before the income-tax bite, too. But Papa couldn't wait for the oil checks to come in each month; he had too many projects going, and a man couldn't do Big Things with Small Sums. He didn't have to look far to find a friendly banker who took the oil wells for security and lent Papa money in respectable hunks of twenty-five thousand and fifty thousand dollars. I was much too young then to argue interest costs with Papa, but I doubt if it would have made any difference. I know what he would have answered. Money was meant to be spent. "I don't drink. I don't smoke. I don't gamble. I don't chase women." Compared to those vices a few thousand dollars a year in interest was almost a virtue.

I sometimes sit at the window and pull at my ear lobe and wonder if maybe I couldn't have squirreled away a little of that glorious bonanza had I been old enough to be Chancellor of the Exchequer then instead of later. Now when the few remaining wells (which no longer flow wildly, but pump fitfully) make even a four-hundred-dollar car-repair bill the proximate cause of nervous indigestion, I muse wistfully on what I might have been able to salvage. Could I have talked him out of the silos perhaps? Or the forest of Chinese elms? Or the tennis courts? Or the flagpole? Of course not! Wasn't it I who gave him the money to tear out the old fireplace and build three new ones to keep him from losing his mind with grief when Mama died? Who stood by unprotestingly during the building of the patio-porch with all those casement windows . . . and who said nothing when Papa built the Highway 66 garage below the porch? And last year, when there was $450 left in the checking account, who wrote out a check for $525 so that

Papa could redesign the entrance to the driveway? Once a person becomes adjusted to money as only a medium of exchange, he doesn't quibble about it.

Oh, when things got really rough, I'd try beating my head against the stone wall of Papa's logic and ask, "Why didn't you ever *save* anything for a rainy day? With all that money coming in, you didn't save a dime. You were too shortsighted, Papa."

"Too *short*-sighted or too *long*-sighted?" Papa said indignantly. "Don't condemn your old Daddy, that way, boy. If I'd put my money in savings it would have been lost. The banks in Sapulpa failed and everybody lost their savings. Two of the banks were held up by outlaws and went broke that way. Yep! The banks collapsed, the stock market crashed, people lost everything they'd saved up— one way or another. At least I have something to show for my money! I have the land and the improvements. It was a blessing I never put money in savings. A *blessing!*"

Argue with Papa!

I learned from my father that being rich had nothing to do with possessing money. Being rich was a state of mind. If the money wasn't in the bank you figured your assets from other sources. We had The Land. Therefore, we were rich. When times got hard and it was touch and go just paying the taxes on all those acres, Papa would drum his powerful propaganda into our ears every day: "Never forget, children, you're rich! You own more than a million dollars' worth of land . . . not to mention the improvements!" We never asked by what inflated yardstick he reckoned the worth of the land. Why put a dollars and cents value on land you had no intention of selling? If it was worth a million dollars to Papa, it was worth a million dollars period.

When you live all your life around somebody who feels rich, the feeling rubs off on you and you feel rich, too. We felt rich when we had the tennis courts, the riding horses, the big Cadillac, and the Pierce-Arrow convertible. But what is more important, we felt rich when the tennis courts were an acre of weeds, the horses had become cow ponies, and the cars were dented and dated. It was the *potential* that made us rich. What we had was unimportant. What we *felt* we had was vital. Why, every acre of rocky, unplowed, unfenced land might still have a million barrels of oil under it!

So we were rich, and we never stopped being rich, and we have Papa to thank (or blame) for this attitude. When you feel rich you can get away with almost anything. You can half-sole the half soles. You can wear patched trousers and a buttonless sport shirt into the bank and pass the time of day with the president in his paneled office. He doesn't feel rich because his standard of values is wrong. He measures his own wealth against the wealth of others. That is his big mistake. He doesn't have the proper feeling for what is his. So he buys Ethyl for his new Lincoln and feels insecure. You buy the cheapest grade of white gas for your old Cadillac and feel rich. He eats a two-dollar luncheon and tries to prove something. You have a stand-up vegetable plate (without the plate) at the produce corner of the Farmer's Exchange and you feel like a king. (You break a banana from a nearby stalk for dessert just because you feel like it.)

This conviction of richness can make you positively insufferable to those who are rich only in money. Papa could smell it when people tried to pull their rank on him simply because they had more money in the bank than he did. He'd suddenly shoot up thirty feet, and from his great height he'd look down on them. His buttonless shirt became cloth of gold. I've seen it happen just this way. I've seen Papa stare down a billionaire and make him feel like a bum. I've seen him do it so many times that I've learned how to do it myself. Papa hammered it into our heads until it became a part of us. "You're rich!" he repeated over and over again. "Don't ever forget that you're rich!"

We never forgot it.

4. PAPA AND RELIGION

Papa spoke Yiddish with an Arkansas accent. One of Papa's distant relatives, who dropped in for a week on his way from New York to California, said to me, "I wish your father would stick to English. When he talks Yiddish he sounds like a Frenchman speaking Italian that he learned from a Swede." His Yiddish was to Yiddish what Yiddish is to German. He had little opportunity to hear Yiddish spoken, but when he did hear it he plunged into the conversation like a long-lost brother. The people he interrupted were considerably startled at this sudden torrent of pidgin Yiddish from what was surely a full-blooded Osage Indian. More than once, Papa's size was the only thing that saved him.

Papa never remembered anyone's having taught him to speak Yiddish, nor to read Hebrew. "I just absorbed 'em," he said. "Picked 'em up along the line."

Hebrew scholars who suddenly heard Papa's voice reading Hebrew prayers looked shocked and disbelieving. On the other hand, we who knew no Hebrew at all marveled at Papa's seeming ability to hold his own with the others. Our prayer books had English on one page and Hebrew on the opposite page. Since those who prayed in Hebrew went faster than those who read the English, we children were always falling behind. During services, we'd constantly call Papa to us and demand to know the correct place at that moment. He'd look at us solemnly, moisten his index finger, and start flipping the pages of the prayer book we handed him. He'd turn ten pages ahead, then back up fifteen. Hopelessly lost, he'd peer over the shoulders of an old-timer who knew where he was, glance at the page number, turn our book to the proper page, and hand it back to us with the pious admonition, "For Pete's sake, try to pray faster!"

My father believed in God, in prayer, and in doing right. Although he knew little if anything about the service itself, he preferred the Hebrew Orthodox manner of worship to the Reform service in English. He was a good observer He stood when others stood. He sat when they sat. He wore his tallith on his shoulders and his yarmulka on the back of his head. During the responsive readings he chanted aloud in that quaint, queer Hebrew vernacular which was all his own. He was proud to be accepted as a fellow member by this group of deeply religious men.

"Do you understand what they're saying?" I asked him once.

"Do I have to understand to be blessed?" he hedged.

"What I mean is—wouldn't you get more out of it if you read the service in English the way the Reform Jews do?"

"Certainly not!" Papa stated emphatically. "The Orthodox Jews are the only real Jews. They pray the way the prayers were written to be prayed. They are religious because there are three hundred and sixty-five things they *can't* do. They can't eat pork. Can't mix milk with meat. Can't eat shrimp. Can't eat catfish. Can't ride on Saturday. Can't do lots of things. And by golly, they are happier *not* doin' all those things than the Reform Jews are who do anything and everything they please! Show me a man whose religion keeps him toein' the mark and I'll show you a good, moral, God-fearin' person. It's when the Church gets so liberal that a member can do anything short of killin' with a clear conscience that the folks in it get into trouble."

Papa compromised, however, on the house of worship he built in Sapulpa. He made it possible for both Orthodox and Reform Jews to hold services in the same place. On high holy days, the Orthodox group began at seven in the morning and took an intermission from ten until noon. During this period the Reform worshipers trooped in and held their services in English. Then the Orthodox resumed their prayers until an afternoon break, when the Reform element took over again. Papa, who felt a Reform service was better than no service at all, stayed through it all.

When Papa first came to Oklahoma, he and Mama made what was then the long trip to Tulsa for the Jewish holidays. They had to choose a hotel close enough to the shul for them to walk to the services because Papa held to the Orthodox belief that it was a sin to ride in a car on holy days. This meant that they had to arrive at the temple early in the morning, kill time between services, and stay until the closing prayers at sundown. Then they walked back to the hotel and began the drive home. Four children complicated this system to the point where religion was almost a chore.

After taking a one-man poll of all elements in the county—strict Orthodox, Conservative, semi-Reform, strict Reform—Papa was convinced that there'd be a willing Jewish congregation right there in Sapulpa if they had a place to pray. He had his eye on a large corner lot (which was two blocks from his house on Oak Street—a short walk to food after a fast day!), and without consulting anyone but himself, he bought it. He then designed one of the strangest temples imaginable. From the street it looked like a neat, comfortable home. Indeed, the front door opened into what was a living room during the non-religious days and a reception room for the congregation on the three or four holy days of the year. The five-room house took up one side of the structure. The other side, which also opened onto the living-reception area, was a temple, large enough to accommodate a hundred worshipers. The walls were always neatly papered, the woodwork freshly painted. There was a rostrum at one end containing a large raised prayer table. The east wall contained an enclosure which held the Holy Torah. The pews were highly varnished pine benches.

Papa was the autocrat of this little temple. His was the responsibility for keeping it clean. He made decisions about repairs. He decided when new prayer books should be purchased. He listened to members' complaints on every subject from too-soft soap to too-hard seats.

It was Herschel Cohen who brought up the subject of the seats.

"Max," Herschel said, "it's not fault that I'm finding. Believe me, we're all loving the shul you built. It's very nice."

"But—" Papa anticipated.

"But maybe the seats are too hard. We all know what Mrs. Shapiro thinks of them. She tells everybody about her piles. But Irving and Rose Brodsky have rear-end trouble, too. Irving tells me that Rose had to leave in the middle of the Rosh Hashana service because she couldn't sit on that wood a minute longer."

"I *like* the benches," Papa said. "A temple doesn't have to sit like a movie."

Herschel pressed his point. "*Your tokis* is well padded, Max. You've got a natural cushion. You must look at the situation from all viewpoints."

Papa couldn't help smiling. "All viewpoints! Front, rear, top, and bottom! O.K., Herschel. You win. I'll have some cushion pads made. We don't want any backsliders just because the seats are too hard on their backsides!"

The cushions not only helped increase the attendance. They made for a happier flock.

When strangers entered this bright and cozy place of worship, with its chintz curtains and its austerely clean look, they got a homey feeling. This was exactly the impression Papa wanted them to get. "A temple should be like a home," he said, "because the Lord lives there." Papa's temple was compared at various times to everything from a small Congregational meetinghouse in New England to a prayer room in Israel. Among churches it was unique.

Papa footed the bill for the works—the lot, the house-temple, the modest furnishings, the prayer books, and the Holy Torah itself.

"It'll always be easy to find a nice couple to live in the house part," he said, "a man and his wife who won't mind our usin' their livin' room three or four times a year. We'll make the rent so low they'll stay a long time and keep the place nice. Won't be any taxes to pay because it's a church. The rent money will take care of the upkeep."

"Dues and fees" was a subject Papa expounded on with great feeling. "I've noticed that they do one tenth prayin' and nine tenths beggin' in a lot of churches," he said. "People don't need to be browbeaten into givin' to the Lord. They hate like hell to put it on a pay-as-you-pray basis. It burns a man up when someone tells him how much he oughta give to his church. The kibitzers who do it confuse themselves with Solomon! Once our little temple gets to goin' it won't cost anybody anything to come and worship God. It'll be plain-lookin' enough so's people won't have to feel that they have to dress up in fancy clothes just to enter it."

Through the years it worked the way Papa planned it. The structure is still there, surrounded by giant trees, landscaped with shrubs (from the Max Meyer Nursery). What a rare temple it was! Free of debt from the beginning. Free of controversy, too. Nobody got mad, nobody resigned, nobody got upset—not even when Papa went for red-white-and-green candy-striped wallpaper (which was a trifle unsettling as you prayed on an empty stomach on Yom Kippur). It was, and still is, a very pleasant place to come to and be with God.

News of Papa's temple spread to all the small towns in the area. People who felt they could not afford the city temples where there were fixed prices for seats, and where most of the worshipers were expensively dressed, came to Sapulpa to worship in the little house-temple, temple-house. There was no choir, there were few trimmings, but everyone who came to pray went away with a good feeling.

Complications occasionally presented themselves, but people rose above them. On Yom Kippur, while the men fasted and prayed, small children ran up and down the narrow middle aisle between the benches eating bananas, apples, and bread-butter-and-jelly sandwiches. Sometimes stone-deaf Teresa Braunstein, who went to the Christian Science Church fifty weeks a year and to the Sapulpa Jewish Temple the other two, carried on a toneless conversation with her cousin Sadie which drowned out completely the voice of the person leading the Reform service. Sometimes old Mr. Finkelstein decided to stay in his seat through the Reform service after leading the Orthodox prayers. He read aloud from his own prayer book (in Hebrew) while the Reform leader valiantly read against him (in English).

But, all in all, it was, and still is, more of a house of worship than many religious edifices infinitely more beautiful, more comfortable, and more financially embarrassed.

The entire congregation was unnerved the Yom Kippur Bea chose to elope with Harold Miller. Three times Harold had come to Sapulpa from St. Louis to ask for Bea's hand in marriage. Three times Papa had put him off. When Bea went back to enroll for her senior year at the university, she enrolled at the Marriage License Bureau instead and telephoned the tidings to Papa the night before Yom Kippur Eve.

Yom Kippur, the Day of Atonement, is a fast day. Jewish people fast from sundown the night before to sundown on Yom Kippur. Papa was so upset at what his daughter had done that he began what amounted to a hunger strike. He ate no supper the night Bea called. Nor did he eat breakfast, dinner, or supper the next day. All during the services he stayed apart, glowering and grieving over the elopement. No one in the congregation dared congratulate him. Mama, who was happy for Bea and knew that the marriage was good, told everyone, "Leave him alone. He'll get over it."

At the end of the Yom Kippur fast Papa had gone without food for two and a half days instead of the conventional twenty-four hours. Mama finally took one of her rare, but effective, stands.

"Max," she said, "if you go around looking like that one more day people will think our daughter has really done something wrong."

"How do I know she hasn't?" Papa muttered. "Elopin' like that without tellin' anybody!"

"They both tried to tell you for three years that they wanted to get married. You wouldn't listen. They are two normal young people in love. Now get to that telephone and call them up at the hotel in Chicago and tell them you forgive them."

"I'm not goin' to do it."

Mama didn't answer him. She went to her closet and started taking out her dresses. She called the children and told us we were going on a trip.

"What's the matter with *you?*" Papa asked uneasily.

"Nothing's the matter with me," Mama said quietly. "I'm not living another day with a man who goes to the temple and prays all day on Yom Kippur and then hasn't an ounce of forgiveness in his heart for his own daughter. I'm going to Texas and I'm taking the children with me." She paused. "I don't think I'll ever come back."

Papa called Bea and Harold that evening. He ate a big bowl of chicken soup first.

If Papa sometimes fumbled the ball on the religious front, he never made a misstep where superstitions were concerned. When it came to being superstitious, Papa was fundamentally pure pagan. He practiced diligently every superstition he ever heard of. When he encountered a new one, he adopted it without question.

Such elementary superstitions as throwing spilled salt over the left shoulder, knocking wood, side-stepping stepladders, coddling mirrors, and avoiding the number thirteen were automatic reflexes with him. He used them so long they were built in.

Once, on our way to Tulsa, Papa made a ten-mile detour because a black cat raced across the highway in front of his car. Bea, who was in a hurry to get to a party, said, "Oh, Papa, keep on going. *Please*. That cat wasn't all-black."

"No, it wasn't," Pearl chimed in. "I'm absolutely positive I saw a white spot on its tail."

"It was almost *gray* instead of black," Manny argued.

Mama said nothing. She knew exactly what Papa would do and she didn't waste her breath. The cat looked all-black to him, and he wasn't taking any chances. Ten miles was a small enough sacrifice when one considered all the terrible things that could happen on the highway.

I suspect that Papa believed in black magic, hexes, and counterhexes. I never found dolls with pins stuck in them, but it is possible they were around if only I'd known where to look.

One of his most rigidly enforced superstitions was Don't Whistle in the House. I never learned where this phobia originated, nor what dire end awaited one who flouted it. But when anyone whistled indoors Papa had conniption fits. Indoors included the car. It included the open-air sleeping porch. It included the porte-cochere adjoining the porch of the Big House. You could sing to your heart's desire, but you couldn't whistle. No, I take that back. Papa was also superstitious about people singing, especially when they sang at the table—particularly in the morning.

("Sing before breakfast, Sonny, and you're sure to cry before supper.")

Another strictly enforced edict was Never Sit on a Pillow. You could sleep on a pillow, lie on a pillow, and have a pillow to warm your feet when you slept under a feather bed on Papa's open porch. But you could never *sit* on one. Sit on a cushion? Yes. On a pillow? No.

Nor could you walk around in your stocking feet. Barefoot? Absolutely. With shoes on? Of course! Bestockinged? No!

Strictly taboo was a hat on a bed. When guests came to visit us and threw their hats and coats on the bed in a bedroom, Papa was on needles and pins until he could sneak in and remove all hats to chairs, tables, or dressers. Coats? Yes. Hats? No. Women's hats? Maybe. Men's hats? Never!

Any plan involving the future had to carry the words "if nothing happens." Future plans of considerable consequence bore the handle "if I *live* and nothing happens." Those words were a sort of oral touch-wood which appeased Papa's gods. They kept planes from falling, tires from going flat, picnics from being rained out.

Papa passed along to his children this "if nothing happens" superstition—probably by environment, but conceivably by heredity. If one of us got negligent and said, "Tomorrow we're going to the football game," or, "Next week we're leaving for Texas with Mama to visit the Levys," Papa would frown, knock wood (or a reasonable facsimile), and caution, "You mean *if nothing happens* you will!" Immediately the child would rephrase the statement to include the proper words. To this day I say "if nothing happens" when discussing plans for the future. The phrase takes most people by surprise because things usually *do* happen. It's when I go all out and invoke Papa's super-special "if I *live* and nothing happens" that I detect an edging-away-from-me trend on the part of the listener.

Papa spat! He spat constantly. He'd spit when anyone mentioned death, dying, incurable disease, or personal misfortune. He'd spit whenever he saw an ambulance, a hearse, or a funeral procession. He'd spit when he heard the name of someone he hated. He would sometimes try to make it appear that he was spitting out a piece of loose filling. Sometimes he'd hide behind a handkerchief. But if it came to a choice of having to be caught spitting or not to spit at all, he spat.

Just as "if I *live* and nothing happens" was more efficacious than merely "if nothing happens," the sounds *ptui-ptui-ptui* added to one or more spits were extra insurance against the thing you were spitting against. Papa used *ptui-ptui-ptui* only in dire emergencies. If it was late at night and the road was bad, and Papa saw a car pulled over to the side of the road he immediately said *ptui-ptui-ptui* and did a spit-spit-spit. Because of some grief he had had from a Nash he once owned, he spit automatically whenever he saw a Nash anywhere.

Whenever Papa spat, we children followed suit. A lot of saliva was expectorated on an overland trip, a lot of it in vain, I fear. Needless spitting and *ptui-ptui-ptui*-ing bothered me. "Papa," I said, "maybe that car parked on the shoulder isn't having trouble at all. It's so dark you can't see whether the tire's flat or the battery's dead or—"

"Look straight ahead," Papa commanded. "If they aren't havin' trouble now, sure as shootin' they're headed for trouble in the future!" Then, after a moment's reflection, he said, "Sonny boy, you talk too much."

It would be unfair and, in a manner of speaking, disloyal to Papa if I didn't admit that spitting and *ptui-ptui-ptui*-ing have seen me through more than one crisis and have staved off almost certain disaster.

Last summer, limping back to Oklahoma with my wife and children after a deluge of car trouble in New Mexico, we reached the point where one more generator failure or water-pump flare-up or hydromatic slip would be the end; we'd all get out of the car and start hitchhiking. And then I remembered Papa's system. Whenever I saw a car pulled over onto the shoulder of the highway, I'd spit three times and say *ptui-ptui-ptui*.

"What in heaven's name are you doing?" my wife demanded.

"I'm working with the odds," I said. "I'm trying Papa's way of holding out when all seems lost. If I spit and *ptui-ptui* at adversity, I'll keep adversity away. It's that simple."

"Why, that's the most ridiculous thing I've ever heard," my wife said.

"I agree," I answered. "But it works."

The two children (chips off their grandfather's block) fell into the mood immediately. They acted as lookouts for cars that were stalled, ailing, or just resting alongside the road. In unison the three of us said *ptui-ptui-ptui* and went spit-spit-spit at each one.

My wife was indignant. "It sets a bad example for the children," she said. Since she had no blood tie to Papa I couldn't expect her to understand.

But late that night, when she was driving the last fifty miles and I was supposed to be asleep, I could have sworn that I saw her spit three times and intone a soundless *ptui-ptui-ptui* as she passed a hapless motorist changing a flat by the side of the road.

In less than an hour we were home . . . high and dry in more ways than one.

5. HOW TO CRACK A SAFE

Mama was a Levy from Taro, Texas. She was the favorite daughter of Philip Levy, who owned more than his share of Taro, a sleepy, complacent satellite of Dallas. The Levys lived comfortably on their own street, Levy Avenue, and owned the largest store in Taro, which Philip Levy had founded in 1860. This store, plus his hundreds of acres of rich Texas black land, supplied the money Philip Levy needed to indulge his tastes in music and drama. He built his own opera house on the second floor of the Levy Building, above his store, and booked every opera and stock company that played Dallas for a one-night stand in his own theater. The seven Levy children sat with their parents in the first row at each opera-house production. Even as a small girl, Mama shared her father's love for the plays of Shakespeare, and Philip Levy would book any play of Shakespeare's except *The Merchant of Venice*. He objected violently to the character of Shylock. "Why should a race of people stand in a bad light because of the acts of one man?" he asked. "The Jews are a generous people. Shylock is the exception that proves the rule." There was nothing of Shylock in Philip Levy. He gave generously toward the construction of every church in Taro long before such contributions were deductible from the income tax.

Mama's front-row exposure to Shakespeare stayed with her when she grew up. Instead of singing lullabies to her babies (she couldn't carry a tune), she drawled Juliet's balcony speech or Polonius's advice to Laertes or Antony's oration over Caesar's body. Long before we knew that we were quoting Shakespeare we blithely told guests that Mama's famous "boardinghouse hash" contained "eye of newt and toe of frog, wool of bat and tongue of dog." When Harold Miller came to Sapulpa from St. Louis the first time to ask for Bea, Manny, who was ten years old, whispered to Pearl, "He has a lean and hungry look." Our standard retort to something we didn't believe was to call it a "tale told by an idiot," and in fact my third-grade teacher sent me home from Washington School with a note which claimed that I had called her an idiot to her face. Mama walked me back to school and convinced her that I was merely quoting Shakespeare and meant nothing personal.

Philip Levy alternated his vacations between steamer trips from Galveston to New York and "a course of baths" at Hot Springs. It was on one of these trips to Hot Springs that Max Meyer, a tall, broad-shouldered, young man about town met Annie Levy, who had just been graduated from Kidd Key College, a Texas finishing school for young ladies. Max, who liked to think he could have any girl he went after in Arkansas, fell in love with this Texas beauty. Annie was diminutive, but gave the impression of strength not frailty. She had brown eyes that sent out special messages to Max and long eyelashes that helped keep those messages private. Her tiny waist intrigued Max. He had an uncontrollable urge to put his huge hands around that waist to see if his finger tips would touch as he encircled it. He didn't dare experiment with this idea until he and Annie were alone in a horse-drawn buggy at the far end of Levy Avenue in Texas some weeks later. Of course it worked. His fingers touched and Annie hardly held her breath at all!

That trip to Hot Springs changed many plans. The Levys had supposed that Annie would marry a somewhat older, already settled bachelor in Dallas who had intimated that he had a question to ask as soon as graduation was over. They reckoned without this Hot Springs flash who whispered his question in Annie's ear the minute he fell in love with her. Philip Levy cut his course of baths short and took his family back to Taro, but the damage had been done. "It's not that I dislike him," Philip Levy said to his daughter. "It's just that he's—well, *different* from us." Mama found that difference exciting.

On his first visit to Texas Max stayed in Dallas and came to Taro on the interurban. Mama and her brother Ed met him at the station and took him to the Levy home for breakfast. His first jolt was the sight and smell of bacon on the table. He made a mental note that his mother must never know that he was in love with a girl whose family not only served bacon, but went for second helpings of it. Subsequent jolts came from other foods the Levys ate with gusto, although forbidden to Orthodox Jews: fried oysters, shrimp, frogs' legs, and even catfish.

The Levy boys were pleasant enough but their college degrees and liberal allowances accentuated the "difference" between them and Annie's boy friend. Morris was a lawyer, Sam was musical, and Ed worried a lot about making more money. Max had little to offer on any of these fronts.

"I don't fit in here, Annie," he confided. "Your folks make me feel like my collar's chokin' me. If it weren't for you I'd high-tail it back to Arkansas in a minute. I never knew anybody before that lived on a street with their own name on it."

Annie laughed. "I'll tell you a secret, Max. It used to be called Asylum Avenue because the state institution is at the end of it. We petitioned to have the name changed, and there were so many Levys living on the street that they called it Levy Avenue."

This explanation comforted Papa, and possibly inspired him to start a namesake community of his own a few years later after he and Mama moved to Oklahoma. There was a tiny settlement named Kellyville that nestled serenely at the south end of the ranch which Papa had bought the same year he moved to Sapulpa. Convinced that Kellyville would grow as Sapulpa and Tulsa were growing, Papa bought all the land east of "downtown" and created a "residential district" of his own. He called it the Max Meyer Addition to Kellyville, and that is the way this land

appears today on the county tax rolls. There was Pearl
Street, Beatrice Street, Manny Street, and Lewis Street
for his four children. There was Annie Avenue for Mama
and Rose Lane for Papa's mother. Since he had lent his
name to the subdivision as a whole, he modestly declined
to name a street for himself. He made Mama very happy
by calling a rough area at the far east end of the subdivision
Philip Park after her father. A few years later, one of the
largest oil wells in the prolific Kellyville pool was brought
in on the rocky terrain of Philip Park. "Something will
come of nothing," Mama said, rephrasing King Lear.

As it turned out, Kellyville refused to grow. Weeds took
over the namesake streets, and only the original signposts
whose paint had flaked and peeled told the story of Papa's
real-estate venture. We children and our chums would
ride horseback across the big meadow, cut through what
was supposed to be Philip Park, and point out to our
friends the signposts with our names on them. We kept on
doing this long after the streets were little more than
cowpaths. Papa seemed to have a closer feeling toward the
Levys after his Kellyville fling. The Levys had only one
street to their credit. Papa had a whole subdivision!

Levy Avenue in Taro kept its hold on Mama long after
she had left it for raw, new, dusty Oklahoma. She missed
the luxury and the family gatherings. She missed the
oysters, too—and the frogs' legs, the shrimp, the catfish,
and the bacon. She'd get jumpy and restless after a few
months of Oklahoma living, and Papa would know that
she needed a refresher course in one of the big houses on
Levy Avenue. He told it this way: "I'd say, 'Go to Taro

for a few days, honey. You need a change.' She'd bundle you kids up and reserve a stateroom on the Frisco. You'd be met in Dallas the next mornin' by some of the Levy retainers, and you'd stay there for a week or ten days. Then I'd call your mother on the telephone and tell her I'd dirtied the last cup and saucer in the cupboard and that the sink was stopped up from old coffee grounds. Next mornin' I'd go down to the depot just to see who was on the train comin' in from Texas, and, sure enough, there'd be your mother and you kids, and she'd ask me how I knew she was comin' and I'd lie and say the Levys had called and begged me to get Annie away from there quick—and we'd both laugh all the way home."

Papa knew what it was to live on somebody else's street. After his marriage, he and Mama lived in Philip Levy's house on Levy Avenue in Taro, and Papa went every morning to the Levy Store—where his collar grew tighter and tighter. An explosion between Papa and the Levys was inevitable, and when it happened it was nuclear. It was not until many years later, however—when I probated my mother's estate after her death—that I learned about the incident which triggered that explosion. In determining what my mother had owned in her lifetime, it was necessary for me to study Philip Levy's will. This document supplied the key to the mystery of why Papa and Mama left tree-lined Levy Avenue for treeless Oklahoma. The will stated emphatically that whatever interest Annie Levy Meyer had in Philip Levy's estate could under no condition be transferred nor willed to her husband, Max Meyer. As a result of the unequivocal wording, all of Mama's interest in the Levy estate passed to her children. Papa got nothing.

I summoned Papa to my office for the express purpose of discovering once and for all why his father-in-law had made such a will. "Sit down, Papa," I began, "and tell me the truth. Why was Philip Levy so determined to cut you out of his estate without a penny?"

Papa squirmed uncomfortably, picked up a couple of letters on my desk and read them, and finally said, "There are some things children don't need to know about their parents."

"I'm not a child any more," I reminded him. "I know that Philip Levy was boiling over when he drew up this will. *Why?*"

Papa looked down at his hands. Perhaps he was remembering how they had encircled Mama's waist all those years before. He clasped his fingers, unclasped them, and said, "Sonny, whatever your grandfather did, it was my fault. I played a practical joke on him and it backfired. I've always been kind of ashamed of myself for what happened. Are you positive you want to know the story?"

"Positive."

"Well, in the Levy Store, which was sorta the meetin' place for the whole tribe, there was a safe. It was the largest safe I've ever seen. A man could walk around inside it without havin' to duck his head. It was a wonderful thing, that safe, and I couldn't get it out of my mind.

"When I got back from my honeymoon, I was supposed to be workin' in the Levy Store. I was on the payroll, but they wouldn't give me anything to do. I about went crazy. If I'd criticize the way they stacked the men's suits on tables, one suit on top of the other, Ed or Morris or Sam would inform me that Levys had been stackin' men's suits one on top of another since 1860—and how long had *I* been stackin' 'em?

"I couldn't take this kind of treatment indefinitely. I was too full of devilment. I wasn't twenty-five yet. I was just married. And I was bored. I was bound to get into mischief, and the safe gave me an opportunity.

"Philip Levy never trusted me with the combination to the safe. All the others—even the bookkeeper—knew it, but not me. When the Old Man would open the safe, he'd shield the combination with his free hand just to keep me from learnin' it. That didn't help my morale any.

"I just naturally gravitated to that safe every chance I got. Once, I was standin' near it and your grandfather showed me a locked drawer inside it. Somewhere along the line some Levy had lost the key to that drawer and it hadn't been opened in years. It hadn't occurred to any of the Levys that a letter to the safe company with the number of the safe and the location of the drawer would fetch a new key to fit it. I copied down the number, wrote the company on Levy Store stationery, and got the key by return mail.

"With the key to the locked drawer for a starter, I put my plan into action. I kept hangin' around your Uncle Ed when he'd open the safe. Ed was so nearsighted he had to get up close and concentrate on his twirling. It didn't take me long to learn the combination by peeking over his shoulder.

"I picked a time when everybody was in the store—all the boys and my father-in-law. I walked back toward the safe and as Ed started to open it, I said, 'Hey, Ed, let *me* try to open that safe today. I'm a pretty good safe opener by Hot Springs standards.'

"Ed sensed that something spectacular was going to happen and he called everybody back to the safe. They all stood around me in a half circle.

"I got onto my knees and blew on my hands the way professionals are supposed to do. I put my ear up to the safe as I turned the dial, actin' like I was listenin' for clicks to guide me. On the last number, I turned the handle and, sure enough, the safe door swung open.

"Nobody said a word. Ed's eyes were poppin' out of his head. Then I pulled about two dozen keys out of my pocket and said, 'You folks just don't know *safes!* I'll bet I've got a key right here in this bunch that'll open that little old locked drawer.' I pretended to study 'em for a minute and then fished out the new key, opened the drawer, turned around, and laughed.

"Nobody else even smiled. Your grandfather was as white as a sheet. He gave me a look I'll never forget and dashed out of the store. He ran the two blocks to his lawyer's office. In ten minutes flat he had dictated me out of his will, his estate, his store—and, as it turned out, his town.

"I never bothered to tell 'em the truth. They wouldn't have believed me, anyway. They went through the years thinkin' that their beloved Annie had married a safecracker from Arkansas. I felt so bad over the way the joke turned out, I forgot to look inside that darned locked drawer. I still don't know what was in it."

"Did Grandpa Philip ever talk about the safe?" I asked.

"Never a word. He acted like it never happened. But right away he started praisin' Oklahoma as the land of opportunity, and suggestin' that maybe I'd like to settle down there and have a store of my own, which he'd be glad to finance. I'd cooked my goose with all of 'em. They wanted to get rid of me no matter how much it cost."

Papa was quiet for a minute. I knew he was preparing to moralize. "Y'see, Sonny boy? See what happens when a feller starts actin' too big for his britches?"

"But, Papa," I protested. "You didn't do anything *wrong*. The Levys just didn't have a sense of humor!"

"Thanks, Sonny," he said, with genuine appreciation. He got up, stretched, and walked out of my office, leaving me holding a copy of Philip Levy's will which failed to leave so much as the eye of a newt to his son-in-law.

6. NATURAL STONE

Papa was a compulsive builder. He went on building binges the way an alcoholic goes on drinking sprees. When the urge to construct came over him he was powerless to resist. Appeals to reason were useless. The shortage of money didn't deter him. Nor did the nonessential nature of what he planned to build. When the building bee bit him he got a look in his eye, a tenseness in his body. He was a slave to this uncontrollable habit.

What the bar is to a drinker, the ranch was to Papa. It was a three-thousand-acre building preserve where he had all the room he needed for his periodic eruptions. From his residence, called the Big House, which he built on his first bender, to the island in the lake, which he installed fifty years later, he never stopped adding. Rumpots sometimes swear off and actually overcome their habit. Not Papa.

He didn't want to stop. "When I stop buildin' things you can call the rabbi," he said.

One of his first creations was the barn. It was the largest barn in Oklahoma when he built it forty years ago. It had a huge hayloft for swinging in that made Robert Frost's birches kid stuff by comparison. He realized after the barn was built that he had built it too close to the Big House. Luckily, the prevailing winds were from the south, but when the wind came from the east, the "lake breeze" was intercepted and contaminated by the "barn breeze," which, like the smell of an elementary school, was indescribable. The barn breeze contained the elements of new-mown hay, old-mown hay, new fertilizer, old fertilizer, horse sweat, cow sweat, sour grain, and saddle soap. If someone had put them all together and bottled them and named the resulting perfume "RFD 1," he'd have sold a million bottles to people with a nostalgic yearning for farm life.

When this barn burned down, Papa built a new one in a different design. The new barn had two long wings, each spacious enough to accommodate one hundred milk cows. He joined the wings together with a native stone milkhouse which boasted a handsome gabled roof.

After the Big House and the original barn, Papa conceived the lake and the bathhouse and the silos. Then he dug a deep water well and installed a vast underground network of pipes which brought running water to most of the houses and buildings on the ranch. When the water didn't run, it walked. Often it stopped entirely when the electric pump broke down.

After the silos, Papa dreamed up the chicken houses

(which covered half an acre) and the Dance Pavilion and the tourist camp. Then came service station No. 1 (with a two-story house attached) and the tavern (with a five-room apartment in the rear) and service station No. 2.

These were his major works, his symphonies. In between them, Papa kept himself tuned up by building houses. Along WPA Row, he built six tenant houses, each with a wood-burning fireplace and a native stone outhouse. (This row of houses got its name during Depression days when Papa had his own private WPA setup, inspired by and fashioned after the goverment's relief program.) Between the Big House and the vast chicken area he built a seven-room caretaker's house (which never housed a caretaker). It was equipped with plumbing and two fireplaces and is still the most comfortable house on the ranch. Then there was the Lake House, a stone's throw from the Dance Pavilion. The Lake House commanded a fine view of the lake from its twenty-foot-wide stone porch. In the opposite direction, across the highway from the Big House, was the nursery house, designed as a dwelling for the nursery manager. Since nursery managers seldom stayed more than two months, the nursery house eventually became "the rent house." Papa liked having a rent house because it gave him the excuse to rebuild it completely to suit each new tenant.

Some of his minor binges included the 150-foot flagpole in front of the Big House, the nursery stand, the tool shed, the grain storage bin known as the feed house, the corrals for the riding horses, the tennis courts, the well house, the boat dock, and the barbecue pits. These barbecue pits were all over the place. Some were open; some were closed. Some were asbestos-lined. Some were giants; others were pigmies. All were built for "next to nothing."

Just as a musician has his favorite motif so did Papa have his. It was building with rock. Only he didn't call it "rock"; he called it "natural stone." All of his creations, beginning with the huge, two-story Big House and ending with the wall around the lake, were built with the rocks which were so abundant on the ranch. Papa often pointed to the hill across the highway and said, "There's enough natural stone there to build a dozen cities!" (He, of course, would be the builder of them all.) He had his own rock quarry where the stones were shaped, trimmed, and cut to size. Some of his walls were made from dark, moss-covered, unchiseled stone; others were faced with quarried rock of a light sandstone color. Papa called natural stone the perfect building medium. It never had to be painted and it stood the years perfectly.

Ernie Cooper was Damon to Papa's Pythias. Their friendship was cemented with the desire that every house in the world should be constructed of stone from the foundation to the roof. Papa would design them all, and Ernie would build them. Next to drinking whisky Ernie Cooper loved chiseling stones.

Ernie was also, in Papa's words, "the champeen fireplace-builder of the world." Papa designed and Ernie built fireplaces in everything from the chicken house to the Dance Pavilion. Ernie also built all the barbecue spots on the place. He was famous not only as a builder of barbecue

pits but as a barbecuer of great talent. When Ernie barbecued it was an all-day job. Beef took eight hours. Chickens
took six. The flame never touched the barbecue. The
smoke did the cooking. Ernie's fee was all the beer he could
hold. He was usually well done before the meat was.

Without Ernie Cooper Papa could never have kept
building. Ernie was perfect for Papa because he had no
ambition whatsoever. He asked only plenty of rocks to
chisel on, a modest home, and an immodest amount of
whisky. Papa supplied them all. He became Ernie's financial retainer, his Unemployment Insurance Bureau, his
Social Security Department, his Blue Cross, and his Santa
Claus. Papa bought the Coopers their clothes, their groceries, and their medicines. He paid for Maud's baby,
Ernie Jack, from delivery date to graduation from Oklahoma A and M College. He bailed Ernie out of jail on an
average of once a month for fifty years. When a man loves
wood-burning fireplaces and barbecue pits as much as
Papa did, he does these things cheerfully.

Long before electricity went rural, Papa had his own
power plant, complete with generator, poles, wires, and
light bulbs. He bought light bulbs by the gross. Lights were
strung across the tennis courts, lights surrounded the lake,
lights were all over the Dance Pavilion, and every tenant's
outhouse was well lighted.

It was a perverse electrical system, always breaking
down when it was needed the most. When Papa invited
friends to the ranch for a swimming party or barbecue, he

always extracted promises from every tenant, cowboy, dairy worker, and traveler in the tourist court not to burn lights after 8 P.M. Every room on the place had coal-oil lamps, wicks trimmed, and basins filled, just in case. We children loved it when the lights went out. Games like dominoes and cassino were more fun when played by lamplight.

All of Papa's "systems" were temperamental. It was nothing unusual to turn a spigot in the sink and get only bursts of air. This meant that the pump at the water well was on the blink again. It also meant that the family in the Big House, the workers on WPA Row, and people in the Lake House were pouring water from ten-gallon bottles that were kept filled for such emergencies.

Papa's sewage system, too, was erratic. It was forever stopping up, backing up, and clogging up. Whenever a bathroom crisis arose, the men had the best of it. At bedtime, Papa, my brother, and I stepped out onto the front porch of the Big House. (How intolerably bright the moonlight was! How deliciously fragrant the smell of earth untouched by plow or human hands!) Each would take a side of the porch, and leaning slightly over his respective railing, he'd water the respective shrubbery below. How Mama and my sisters managed without having to leave the house was one of the unsolved mysteries of my youth. I believe it involved chamber pots. Whatever it was, they performed their chore quickly. They were already in bed when the three men came trooping back into the house. Papa then pulled the switch or (more often) blew out the coal-oil lamp, and we all went to sleep.

In front of the Big House was a rare thing—a failure which Papa agreed was a failure: the fountain. The fountain consisted of two cement circles, one inside the other, each about a foot thick and three feet high. Papa intimated vaguely that statuary had been intended within the inner circle, but none ever appeared there. At one point Papa installed a vertical piece of pipe in the center of the fountain. Water was supposed to shoot into the air from this pipe and cascade gently down into the cement circles. He trained an orange spotlight on the pipe for an added effect. However, he underestimated the water pressure. When he turned on the water, everyone sitting near the fountain, and even everyone on the front porch, got drenched with rusty water. This one attempt cured Papa's striving for special effects. He never turned the water on there again.

Occasionally, when someone would ask Papa what in the world those cement rings were, with the odd piece of pipe in the center, Papa's answer depended upon his mood at the moment. Once I heard him say, "They are old Indian ruins—all that's left of a beautiful castle that stood on this spot thousands of years ago. They were the foot baths of the tribal chieftains." Most of the time he'd confess his failure and add, "What you see is only temporary. Someday I'll tear it down and build a *real* fountain." He hasn't got around to doing it . . . yet.

If the fountain was an admitted failure, directly in front of it was one of Papa's greatest successes: the flagpole. The flagpole was the sentry that gave distinction to the ranch. You'd turn into the driveway from the highway, proceed straight ahead until you came to the flagpole, then turn to the right and commence a circle around the house. The Big House was the center of a white-road ring, and the flagpole was the ring's setting.

Embedded into the ground in a tremendous cement block, the flagpole, which was made of galvanized oil-field pipe, shot into the air a full 150 feet. Papa built it, too, for "next to nothing." Whatever it cost, it was worth it. Many a Highway 66 traveler on his way to California was so impressed by it that he stopped at the tavern or filling station merely to ask what retired general or admiral lived in the stone house with the tremendous flagpole.

Papa was extremely conscientious about displaying the flag. Of course he observed all national holidays. He also pulled the flag to the top of the pole on Mama's and the children's birthdays, on Mother's Day, Father's Day, Valentine's Day, and St. Patrick's Day. Other flag-flying occasions were Rosh Hashana and Yom Kippur (Ernie Cooper raised and lowered Old Glory on those days because Papa was busy praying in the shul), and whenever guests were expected. Even today, when my family and I head for the ranch, I find myself straining expectantly as I approach the straightaway. My eyes seek out the flagpole. As soon as I see the flag whipping in the wind, I know that Papa is waiting for us and all is well.

The boys and girls who lived on the ranch liked to take part in the flag ceremonies. Carrying the flag to the flagpole was a rare privilege. So was helping with the folding of the flag after sundown, with Papa on one corner and children on the other three. Everyone stood at attention as the flag went up and came down. The flag which had seemed so enormous on the ground looked very small by the time it reached the top of the pole.

"How big is that flag?" one of the children asked Papa once.

"It's the biggest flag in the U.S.A.," Papa replied with a grin.

We all knew he was joking when he said that, but we believed him nevertheless.

I still do.

I was fourteen when the flagpole painter strolled down our driveway late one summer afternoon, knocked at the front door, and asked to see my father. I double-checked to make sure that the screen was locked, then went to get Papa. We'd been warned against strangers drifting in from the highway.

"Yes?" Papa asked, striding out onto the porch where the man was sitting on the railing waiting for him.

"Just wondered if you'd like your flagpole painted, mister."

Papa studied the frail-looking man in the faded brown, sweat-stained sport shirt and the patched blue jeans. Papa wanted his flagpole painted in the worst possible way, so he said, "It doesn't need paintin', especially."

The stranger was used to this kind of bargaining. "Sure looks bad from here."

"Where you headed?" Papa asked, changing the subject.

"California. I'm broke. I'll paint that there flagpole for ten dollars, mister. Ten dollars and a place to sleep tonight."

Papa was excited and he showed it. Flagpole painters were hard to find at any price and ten dollars was a bargain.

"Have you ever painted a flagpole?" Papa asked warily.

"Dozens of 'em," the stranger replied in a truthful-sounding voice. "Heights don't faze me. I helped paint the George Washington Bridge in New York."

"It's a deal," Papa said. He then appointed Ernie Cooper to take charge of the stranger while he drove into town to buy the paint before the store closed. He had to choose between silver and gold and finally settled on silver.

After supper while it was still light, Papa, Ernie, and the flagpole painter rigged up a painter's seat out of a block of wood. A steel cable was bound to the wooden seat. The other end of the cable was looped through the pulley at the top of the pole. By holding onto this end and backing up or going forward, a person on the ground could hoist or lower the painter on the seat.

"Where'll you start?" Papa asked the painter.

"At the top, of course," the painter replied. "Pull me up to the top and then work me down."

Papa could hardly wait for morning.

Several tenant farmers, their wives, and children were gathered at the flagpole at six the next morning, waiting for the hoisting. Several people from Kellyville came to see the painter, and three or four folks from Sapulpa drove out to the ranch.

The painter secured himself to the wooden seat, handed the cable to Papa, straddled the bucket of silver paint, and said, "Let 'er rip!"

As Papa pulled the cable which sent the painter up, the

painter wrapped his legs around the flagpole. He appeared to be shinnying up under his own power. Finally he reached the top, dipped his brush into the bucket, and started daubing the weather vane with silver paint. He seemed oblivious to the wind which caused the pole to sway back and forth two or three feet. The people on the ground were tense and silent as they watched the painter working away on the bending pole. Beads of perspiration danced on Papa's brow as he held the cable taut while the painter slapped his brush against the pole and slowly inched his way down, leaving a gleaming silver trail behind him.

When the flagpole no longer swayed under the painter's weight the thrill value of the spectacle had disappeared and so had most of the onlookers. By three o'clock no one was left except the painter, Papa, and me. Only thirty feet remained to be painted. Papa lowered the painter to the ground for a drink of water. While he was standing next to me, I said, "Get dizzy up there?"

"Naw," he answered. "Just look at the pole and don't look down and you're O.K. Want to ride up a ways, boy?"

"Can I, Papa?" I asked.

"Sure, just for a little ways," Papa said.

They tied me to the seat and pulled me up about fifteen feet. I began to get seasick. The painter saw me turning green and immediately lowered me to the ground.

"Now how about you?" the painter said, turning to Papa. "Want to have a look at your ranch from up there?"

"Oh, I'm much too big for that small seat," Papa said, liking the idea. "You aren't strong enough to hoist me, young feller."

The painter resented Papa's impugning his strength. "Want to bet?" he asked, maneuvering Papa onto the seat and tying him in.

"That cable's awful thin," Papa protested, half backing away, seat and all.

"It'll hold you fine," the painter insisted, tightening the cable and pulling Papa off the ground. "Sit easy. Relax. I can pull you. The pulley up top does the hard work. I'm stronger than I look."

Papa was already going up the flagpole. For the first few feet he beamed and waved at me. "If I'd known it was this easy, Sonny, I'd have painted it myself!" he quipped. Then he glanced down, gulped, and said, "That's enough. You can let me down now. Easy, boy."

The painter acted as though he hadn't heard. He stepped back and kept pulling at the cable wire, hoisting Papa higher and higher. It was an incongruous sight—so little cable holding so much Papa so high in the air.

"Papa, come *down*," I yelled. "Papa, you're gonna *fall*."

By this time Papa was half way up the flagpole. "Hey! This is high enough. Let me down."

The painter was enjoying it immensely. He gave a fresh tug on the cable wire, sending Papa up another few feet on the pole.

Papa by now was convinced that the painter had lost his mind. He was more angry than scared as he yelled, "Damn it! Let me down this damned pole this minute or I won't pay you one damned cent!" One "damn" from Papa was unusual. Three in a row was unheard of.

Perversely, the painter gave one more pull. Papa started

hugging the flagpole with his arms, embracing it with his legs, and screaming at the top of his lungs, "Help! Help!"

Mama heard the cries in the kitchen. She came running to the front porch, dashed down the stone steps, saw Papa's predicament, and intending his rescue, started beating on the painter with her fists while she shouted, "Let go that rope this minute! Let go that rope!"

When Papa heard that, he almost fainted. "Get *away*, Annie," he yelled. "Do you want him to let me *drop?* Leave him *alone!*"

This seeming bit of ingratitude made Mama so mad that she stopped pounding the painter, looked up at Papa disgustedly, and said, "Go on and *fall* for all I care!" and stormed back into the kitchen.

By this time the painter realized that the joke had gone too far. In just a moment Papa was standing on the ground again, his face and body lathered with sweat, his arms and legs skinned from embracing the pole, and his body silver-streaked from encounters with undried paint.

He tore himself out of the cable, letting the wooden seat fall to the ground. He ran into the house like a wild man, was there only a few seconds, then shot right out again waving a ten-dollar bill. "Here! Take your money. Now, *go!*"

The painter looked sheepish. "What about the rest of the pole?"

"The *hell* with the rest of the pole. *I'll paint it myself!*"

"Aw— I was just having a little fun, mister."

"Fun, my *ass!*" Papa roared. He looked at the frail cable wire still flapping against the pole and shuddered.

After the painter had gone, Papa tried to figure out a way to paint the bottom thirty feet of the flagpole. He offered Ernie Cooper a whole quart of whisky if Ernie'd let Papa hoist him up on the little seat to finish the job. It broke Ernie's heart, but he had to refuse. He couldn't take heights. Ernie did paint from the bottom of the pole up to as far as he could reach standing on a stepladder. The remaining twenty feet went unpainted. Through the years the flagpole gleamed silver from the base up ten feet, then turned black for twenty feet, then silvered again for the 120-foot rise to the top. On a moonlight night, when we sat outdoors in front of the Big House and looked at it, the flagpole seemed to be split into two parts—with nothing but darkness holding them together.

"Maybe you should have let him go ahead and paint the rest of it," I said to Papa one summer night as the two of us were sitting by the fountain enjoying the breeze and studying the flagpole.

"How can you even suggest such a thing?" Papa replied. And then he used one of the few "bad" words I ever heard him say: "Why, Sonny boy, that sonuvabitch could've *killed* me!"

Between his building symphonies, Papa kept in trim by using the Big House for finger exercises. The way some people move furniture, Papa moved walls. At one point he removed a staircase which went to the second floor and built a brand-new staircase three rooms away.

For twenty-five years he had operated on the ranch house by remote control from Sapulpa. We lived in the Big

House in the summertime, moving back to town in the fall. But when he moved to the ranch permanently, Papa tore out most of what he had rebuilt and rebuilt it all over again. He completely redesigned the kitchen—adding three new windows and moving the door. He built a spacious natural-stone porch off the kitchen which he referred to as his "dream porch." The porch contained a wood-burning fireplace, a powder room, a barbecue pit, and 126 casement windows.

This porch, which he built in the 1940's, was financed with what Papa called "found money." The family had gone together to give my brother and his bride a new convertible for a wedding present. When the marriage collapsed after six weeks, the bride insisted on giving the car back to the family, and the family gave the car to Papa. Papa sold the car back to the dealer and converted the money from the convertible to his dream porch. Beneath the porch he built a garage large enough to accommodate ten cars. We called it the Highway 66 Garage.

Papa had several distinguishing trademarks in his home building and rebuilding. The mirror was one. He never hung pictures, preferring to mirror entire walls. All doors had full-length mirrors on both sides. The main living room's north and south walls were completely mirrored. These mirrors made dancing in the large room almost impossible. If you glanced at one of the mirrored walls you saw yourself and your partner reflected back and forth, forth and back, ad infinitum. Inevitably you ended up tripping over each other.

Another trademark was the secret hiding place. Under

the shelves of linen closets in bathrooms were secret drawers. At the bottom of many of his mirrors were long secret chambers with openings at each end. He loved disappearing panels and walls within walls. One of his cleverest hiding places was the liquor storage room behind the wall of the pantry. Because Oklahoma was a dry state then, Papa was always afraid the house would be raided for contraband booze. He knew perfectly well that private homes were never raided, and that even if they were, his wouldn't be. Nonetheless, Papa built his liquor hideaway so skillfully that a harassed bootlegger would give his eyeteeth for one just like it. The walls of this pantry were of grooved wood. On one of the grooves was the tiniest hole. You had to know the hole was there or you could never find it. Into this hole Papa fitted an ice pick, pushed forward, and lifted. The entire panel opened up, revealing a huge storage space behind it. So cleverly was the hole concealed that I often had to search for almost an hour, ice pick in hand, looking for the darned hole so that I could get a drink of whisky.

Another thing that distinguished Papa's houses was bathrooms. "The bathroom is the most important room in the house," Papa insisted. "All other rooms are public. The bathroom's the only place left in the world where a man can retire and know he'll be able to enjoy a little privacy." Papa preferred the term "powder room" to "bathroom." He built so many of these privacy retreats that a guest in the Big House claimed he discovered a powder room with an adjoining powder room.

There were three powder rooms in the basement, one

with walls, the others exposed. "I built three at the same time to get a quantity discount on fixtures," he said. "I figured I could always build walls around them whenever I got hold of some extra material."

There were six powder rooms on the main floor (two of them so successfully hidden that people had difficulty finding them even when told where they were).

Where there were six powder rooms for one bedroom on the main floor, there were six bedrooms for one powder room upstairs. This one was, however, the largest bathroom I have ever seen in any house anywhere. The pink and green tile floor was a mosaic masterpiece worthy of a harem. The walls were tiled halfway up, then mirrored from there to the ceiling. One "wing" of this powder room contained a dressing unit with long marble-topped tables and lights in a brilliant semicircle, obviously inspired by a Hollywood star's dressing room. Another "wing" was devoted to the tub, washbasin, and shower stall. Hidden discreetly (you had to look for it and sometimes found it with no time to spare) was what most people came to the powder room to use.

There was just one drawback to Papa's super powder room. It was without water. His water system was incapable of boosting water to the upper story. He knew that eventually he'd get the pressure he needed—by building a new water tank near the barn with a 100,000-gallon capacity—so he spent the ten-year dry spell making this powder room into a real show place. He succeeded. It was more beautiful than any magazine advertisement for plumbing fixtures. When Papa took guests on a tour of his powder room, he explained casually that the water wasn't available yet for it and they'd have to go downstairs when they wanted a bathroom they could use. Most of the guests said they didn't mind at all. It was too pretty a place to use for anything other than sight-seeing.

The fireplaces were therapeutic. They cured Papa of a bad attack of melancholia. It was an expensive prescription, but it did the trick.

Mama died so suddenly Papa couldn't adjust to the change. His grief stayed new and painful. Mama had been perfectly content to be Papa's audience, his straight man, his silent partner. When he was happy, she was happy. She loved to watch him eat, to hear him laugh, to share him with other people. She had a fanatical loyalty to him that caused her to side with Papa even in his foolishness against her own people and their good sense. Her sustained devotion had been a comforting thing and Papa was bewildered after he was deprived of it.

Bea and Pearl were married, with families of their own. Manny was still in the army. It was I who watched Papa wander from room to room of the house on Oak Street, vainly trying to adjust to loneliness. I wanted to do something for him, but I couldn't think of anything that would interest him. Then I learned about the fireplaces from Papa himself.

"Sonny boy," he began, "we really oughta sell this place in town and move to the ranch."

"Could you stand to sell it, Papa? Could you part with the house and all its memories?"

"The memories will go with me when I move out of it," he said. "That little frame house on the corner of Cedar Street—you know, I've pointed it out to you children a thousand times—your Mother and I lived there when we first came to Oklahoma. Every time I pass that little house on that corner all my memories freshen up. You don't have to stay in a place to be part of it. You can carry it with you wherever you go."

It hurt hearing Papa talk like that. His sadness was everywhere about him. Never before in his life had he been unhappy.

"We'll move to the ranch, Papa. It's only five miles from town. We'll sell this house and settle down in the Big House on the ranch."

"After I rebuild the fireplace," he said cautiously.

"Huh?" I thought I had misunderstood him.

"The fireplace, Sonny boy. A person couldn't think of movin' to the ranch house with that old fireplace bein' as wrong as it is."

"Why, Papa, we don't use the fireplace much with the heating system. It *looks* all right. It's—"

"It's hopeless," Papa said. "I should never have built it on the north in the first place. The new one will be on the east—in the center of the livin' room, opposite the front door. Ern and I have a plan that—"

I was stunned. "Papa! Do you have any idea what it means to build a brand-new fireplace in a house that's already built? A house with two floors and a basement?"

Papa was stirring from his depression. His eyes began to

twinkle as the old building drug started to take effect. "We'll have *three* fireplaces, Sonny. One on the top floor, a bigger one in the livin' room, and another one in the basement."

"But—"

"Ernie and I have been selectin' stones from our very best rock collection. It will cost next to noth—." He stopped. "Well, we might as well face it. It *will* cost *something*." He wilted. "We can't afford it, can we?" He seemed to wither again. "*Can* we?"

I wished my brother and sisters could be there to help me answer him. Nobody knew better than I how strained the family finances were at that moment. Buildings needed repairs. Papa was already agitating for his new 50,000-gallon water tank which we all knew he'd get. Surely this was no time to be spending money tearing out a perfectly good fireplace and building three brand-new ones.

I looked at Papa. Of course he'd survive without his fireplaces. But he'd grow sadder and sadder and sadder. He needed a dose of his building tonic right then or he'd dry up. What he built didn't matter. It could be a greenhouse or a tunnel or an overpass. It just happened to be fireplaces.

"Of course there's enough money," I said. "Go to it, Pop."

The next day Ernie Cooper and his wife moved into the Big House. They lived there for six months until Project Chimneys was completed. Papa directed the tearing out of existing walls, the moving of the staircase (to make way for the new chimney locations), and the choosing of stones.

Some of these rocks were remarkably patterned. In the center of the upstairs fireplace was a rock resembling an open fan—with eroded ridges for dividers and a green moss handle. The central rock in the living room fireplace looked exactly like one of Thurber's dogs.

From near and far people came to see Papa's fireplaces. The tour began on the top floor with the "little one." Papa reached down, pulled up the lid in the center of the hearth, and proclaimed, "Look! An express chute to the basement for ashes!" Then he showed the impressive fireplace in the main-floor living room, preening himself in the compliments. And then he led the way to the basement. Here was without a doubt the largest fireplace this side of hell. Even people who had seen mammoth fireplaces in their time gasped at its size. It was the Atlas of fireplaces, capable of holding all others on its rock mantle. Truly it was the fireplace to end all fireplaces.

Papa confided that "some day—not immediately—but *some* day" he'd go ahead and complete this part of the house. He'd build a room around this fireplace. "Sort of a game room, a rathskeller." Then, if he saw me coming, he repeated loudly, "Not now, of course. . . . Maybe when we strike some more oil. . . ." His face was sunlight. His eyes were stars. His voice was music. He was happy again.

7. CHEOPS IN SAPULPA

If Papa was creative inside houses, he was absolutely monumental on his outside projects. Take the lake, for example. Papa had a set against conventional swimming pools. "Even the largest ones are like concrete bathtubs," he said. "Who wants to share a bathtub with a bunch of strangers? And I might add," he said confidentially, "people *do* things in swimmin' pools they wouldn't do even in their own tubs!"

So when Papa got the idea of having a place to swim on the ranch it was only natural that he came up with a swimming pool six acres in size and dug to order. Most of Papa's buildings were imaginative, free-lance, add-a-little-subtract-a-little-as-you-go affairs. But the lake was engineered. Papa still has the blueprint. It's framed, and it hangs on the wall of his favorite powder room in the basement of the Big House.

Papa selected a pleasant basin-shaped meadow for his swimming pool. It was not too far (but far enough) from the Big House. The long south side of the lake he cleared and covered with sand for a beach. From the beach he sloped the lake gently toward the middle where he built a twenty-one-foot, three-level, three-directional steel diving tower. Toward the east end of the lake, Papa designed the jump-off—a hole hollowed out near the banks, with a water depth of fifteen feet. He placed a small springboard here. How much all this excavating cost, even fifty years ago, Papa never divulged.

Behind the natural-stone wall which circled the lake he built a high bank "wide enough to accommodate a car." Fortunately, no one ever tried to make the trip. It wouldn't have worked. The road was only four feet wide.

Near the beach Papa sank rows of iron pipes which he strung with iron link chains for waders to hang onto. Odd-shaped umbrella-topped iron fountains sprang up from various parts of the lake. They were merely for ornamentation as Papa forgot to hook them up to water lines for the fountain effect he originally planned.

The lake was graveled and sanded near the beach. Elsewhere mud prevailed. More than once I jumped from the top of the high diving tower and sank deep into the soft, gooey mud that held me for a second like a suction cup. Sometimes I panicked lest the mud refuse to release my feet so that I could rise to the surface and breathe again. All of my friends loved to jump from that top board and sink ankle-deep in the mud below. It was a thrilling and awesome adventure.

Despite the mud bottom, the lake was surprisingly clear. Many natural springs helped. You could tell where the springs were when you swam through the ice-cold spots. And even if people did do what they shouldn't have done, Papa pointed out that the sunlight, the vegetation, and the size of the pool took care of everything antiseptically.

The lake was a full three city blocks' distance from the Big House. "Why did you build the lake so far away?" I asked Papa.

"So the swimmers wouldn't run into the livin' room with wet feet," he answered. "People get mighty careless when it's somebody else's pool and somebody else's livin' room. That's why I built a bathhouse down by the lake."

Unless we had too many guests, we children had undressing privileges at the Big House (boys in the basement, girls in the back bedroom on the first floor). Then, in old tennis shoes or barefooted, we picked our way through the dust, rocks, and prickly plants past the barn, past the caretaker's house, past the chicken house, down a dusty road which turned north at the Lake House, and then on down to the beach. Since the barn was almost an annex to the Big House's back porch, we sometimes jumped onto cow ponies we found saddled there and rode them down to the lake in our swimsuits, leaving the horses to graze while we swam.

When large swimming parties used the lake, they changed their clothes in the bathhouse, a functional structure divided into two parts (MEN, WOMEN), each side containing benches, hangers, showers, and other facilities.

Inside the section labeled MEN was a large sign which read:

KINDLY
Do Your Business
Before Entering the Water

YOUR HOST

I spent a good part of my childhood eaten up with curiosity over whether there was a similar sign in the women's
division. It took me years to screw up enough courage to
walk into the part of the building marked WOMEN. I was
twelve years old. I selected a rainy morning when I knew
there wasn't a WOMAN within shouting distance. I looked
in all directions to make sure that no one saw me entering
the forbidden area, then I darted inside. It was disappoint-
ing to find an identical layout to the men's with one
exception. The sign for the more delicate eyes to see read:

A LADY IS ALWAYS NEAT IN EVERYTHING

YOUR HOST

Papa seldom swam in the lake. He had a swimming suit
and we have a picture of him wearing it; however, when
we yelled, "Come on in . . . the water's fine!" (everyone
yelled that in those days), Papa said, "Aw, shucks, anyone
with a stomach as big as mine shouldn't parade himself in
a bathin' suit."

Perhaps Papa had another reason for staying out of the
lake—the fish.

A representative of the State Game and Fish Commission sold Papa on the idea of stocking his lake with fish.

"I'm getting three barrels of minnows absolutely free," Papa announced one night at supper.

"What in heaven's name are you going to do with all those minnows?" Mama asked.

"Why, turn 'em loose in the lake, of course! We'll have the best privately stocked fishin' hole in the country."

"But, Papa," Bea protested, "what about when we're in swimming? If I came face to face with an ugly old fish I'd be scared to death!"

"Don't worry about that," Papa reassured her. "The fish are more afraid of you than you are of them. They'll mind their own business and stay close to the far banks where you kids never swim."

If Papa really thought that the fish in his lake would submit to voluntary segregation, he learned differently in a hurry. A child would be holding onto the iron chain in the shallows, splashing merrily, when suddenly he'd let out a war whoop that brought everyone to him in a hurry. "I *felt* something," he'd say. "Something *bit* me."

Of course the fish didn't bite. Papa assured us that fish *couldn't* bite people. But they did bump. As they grew larger and finnier they gouged and scratched the swimmers they bumped into.

Swimmers are to fishermen what cattlemen are to farmers. In Papa's lake this antipathy was pronounced. The fishermen along the banks accused the swimmers of making too much noise and scaring the fish away. This encouraged the swimmers to splash all the more to *keep* the fish away.

Eventually, but slowly and surely, the fish and the fishermen did win sole possession of the lake. The sandy beach reverted to grass and weeds. The graveled shallow part changed to mud. It looked more and more like a natural lake—except for the iron posts and the chains and the skeletal three-decker tower in the center and the rusted iron fountains with the umbrella tops. In later years, if anyone looked disbelieving when Papa described what the lake had formerly been, he whipped out his blueprint as proof of paternity.

Papa got mad when fishermen used his lake without permission. He posted signs and hired lookouts but intruders kept trespassing. Papa boiled.

"Drive in my front gate! Park in my back yard! Walk down to my lake! Help themselves to my fish!" Papa held both fists up to the sky. "And they don't even bother to say good mornin'!"

Finally, to spite them, Papa decided to let the water out of the lake. He had built a small spillway to handle overflow. Below the spillway was a twelve-inch pipe which could be opened up to let the water flow out into a winding overflow creek which disappeared down the pasture toward Ernie Cooper's stone quarry.

On the Sunday morning that Papa walked down to the lake and counted twenty-three uninvited fishermen—all having extraordinary luck in the by now overpopulated lake—he made his decision. He marched himself to the cutoff, gave the wrench a few turns, and stepped back. Out shot a torrent of water.

When he came back with his wrench a few hours later to close the cutoff, the lake was considerably lower. There was enough water for the fish (although they probably were bumping into each other at that point), but the stone wall was no longer a convenient place for a fisherman to sit, and the soft muddy rims made any sort of footing unattractive.

The rains eventually filled the lake again, but Papa became cutoff-happy. He couldn't control his urge to go below the spillway, open the pipe, and turn his lake into a muddy relief map of its blueprinted original.

When we pressed him for his reasons, Papa told the truth. "At first I did it to chase away the fishermen, but now I do it because I love to see the water swoosh through that big pipe. Don't worry. The spring rains will fill it again soon."

Sometimes the spring rains failed to materialize and the once glorious swimming pool was an ugly mudhole with a spindle-legged diving tower in the middle, iron posts and chains near the muddy beach, and a lone rowboat chained to the dock, resting on the muddy bottom.

The west end of the lake always bothered Papa. "It's too flat," he complained. "There oughta be an island over there." It took him almost forty years to do something about it, but on his seventy-fifth birthday, he and his crew of Indian workers started a project. With the help of a rented bulldozer they began construction of an island. When the island was completed it had a kind of Robert

Louis Stevenson enchantment to it. It was possible to circle the island in a rowboat if you bent very low under the willows at the far end.

"I built it for the grandchildren," Papa said. "They'll have a wonderful time playin' on that island."

To this day only one grandchild has ever dared leave the security of the boat to explore the island. He wasn't gone long. He ran back to the boat, flailing through the weeds and brambles and hinting that he'd "seen something awful," which he refused to describe further.

The island had to be built. It completed Papa's picture of what the perfect swimming pool–fishing hole should look like. And it cost next to nothing.

Papa conceived of the Dance Pavilion, an oversized wooden structure balanced on pillars of natural stone, as a rumpus-room-away-from-home. Here, in this sprawling open-air building, Papa gave hundreds of parties. He was a gracious and generous host, hellbent on seeing that everyone who came had a wonderful time.

The Dance Pavilion made life easier for Mama, too. It was the gesture of a thoughtful husband. "Honey," Papa said to her, "you'll never have to worry about cleanin' up after parties. People won't dirty ash trays because they won't need 'em! They'll just flick their ashes over the railings. No furniture to mar, no floors to wax, no walls to damage. There's not a thing in the Dance Pavilion that can get hurt!"

Guests loved the freedom of the pavilion. They filled their paper plates with barbecue, potato salad, and slaw.

They drank their Cokes straight from the bottle. They sat on the long benches around the side, enjoyed the view of the lake, and tossed their gnawed ribs over the railings into the weeds below.

In a far corner of the open kitchen, hidden under tow sacks, was a tub of iced beer. This belonged to Ernie Cooper, who had created the barbecue pit in the Dance Pavilion. This barbecue pit was Ernie's masonry master-piece. It was so enormous that the hickory logs had to be inserted from outside the pavilion to provide fuel for the meat Ernie cooked on the vast area of grates indoors.

On this tremendous grill Ernie barbecued prodigious quantities of ribs (beef ribs—Papa was anti-pork), roasts, chickens, and turkeys. Guests begged for Ernie's "burnt pieces," charred endpieces which were deliciously succulent and heavenly flavored with the liquid dynamite known as "Max Meyer's Famous Hot Sauce." Ernie basted the meat with this sauce as he cooked it. He served generous portions of the sauce on the side to those whose stomachs were asbestos-lined and who liked it hot.

Every time one of his children graduated from Sapulpa High School, Papa gave a barbecue for the entire school system. All the teachers, principals, their wives, husbands, and children were invited. There was swimming, fishing, and boating for all—and then a huge spread at the Dance Pavilion.

Papa's party always took place two weeks before the presentation of awards to graduating seniors. By the sheerest of coincidences, each of the four Meyer children won the school cup for all-around achievement. My brother and I were the Best All-Around Boys of our classes; my sisters the Best All-Around Girls of theirs. We used to tease Bea, who had an inclination toward overweight, about the all-around part. It made her furious.

I felt guilty about my award and I told Papa so. "Papa, I didn't deserve it."

"Deserve what?"

"The cup for being the Best All-Around Boy. I *wasn't* the best. Icky Allen had me beat for one; Bill Nelson for another."

"Sonny, if you're thinkin' that my barbecue for the school system had anything to do with your cup, you're just bein' unfair to yourself. I'm positive the votin' took place weeks before the barbecue."

I wish I could have been as positive about it as Papa was. My brother and sisters had their doubts, too. It was just too darned coincidental. I associated the awards with the barbecues and developed a mental set against the Dance Pavilion where the crimes were perpetrated. It was the only building on the ranch that gave me a sense of shame. Today, all these years later, when I look at the four silver All-Around cups lined up in a row on the mantle, I still lose my appetite for barbecue.

The Dance Pavilion was the reason Papa resigned from the Downtowners.

Papa was a joiner. He was a Mason, a Shriner, an Elk, a Moose, a Woodman of the World, a Knight of Pythias, and an Odd Fellow. He desperately wanted to be a Knight of Columbus and almost made it. He was a guest at so many of their meetings that a friend submitted Papa's name as an honorary Knight. The local group voted unanimously for him, but the Bishop raised so much fuss about it that Papa had to resign.

The only organization he didn't join was the Ku Klux Klan, and it wasn't for lack of an invitation. When the Klan terrorists were burning fiery crosses and tarring and feathering Negroes, Catholics, and Jews, three of Papa's oldest friends paid him a visit. They locked themselves in the back room of the house on Oak Street and talked for more than two hours.

Mama could hardly wait for them to leave. "What did they want, Max?" she asked worriedly.

"Annie, they . . ." He sat down. "Annie, they want me to be a member of the Ku Klux Klan!"

Mama was thunderstruck. "You're Jewish. The Klan hates Jews."

"I know it. They know it, too. But they want me, anyway. Say they feel like heels keepin' me out of anything they belong to."

"What did you tell them?"

Papa straightened up as he spoke. "I told them that they degrade themselves by persecutin' innocent people while hidin' behind sheets. I told them they were bad Christians and a disgrace to their children. I think maybe they're gonna resign from the Klan tomorrow. I lectured 'em hard!"

Being a Downtowner was different. Papa liked the organization and took an active part in its work and play.

When the Downtowners asked Papa if they could use

his Dance Pavilion for one of their parties, Papa was
delighted. He even threw in Ernie Cooper and a tub of beer.

During the barbecue supper Papa walked up to the Big
House and reported on the good time everyone was having.
"A few of the boys are tipsy," he said to Mama, "but
nobody's hurtin' yet. The casualties will start when the
crap game begins later on."

Around nine o'clock Papa ambled down toward the
Dance Pavilion to observe the game. Papa was a kibitzer
not a participant. When he wanted to gamble he bought
160 acres of land from a map, sight unseen, and forgot
about it until the lease hounds came around. Games left
him cold.

Ten minutes later he came charging back into the house.
His face was fiery-red. He was breathing like a bull. He
had run the whole distance from the Dance Pavilion.

Mama rushed to him. "Max! What's the matter?"

"Naked ladies!" Papa screamed. "They've got naked
ladies down there doin' a show for the Downtowners.
Naked ladies are performin' on *my* Dance Pavilion!"

My sisters wandered into the room to see what was the
matter with Papa.

"Go to bed!" Papa ordered. "Go to bed this minute!"

It was a full hour before their bedtime but they scooted
to bed without an argument.

After they'd gone, Mama said, "Why didn't you tell the
Downtowners to stop the show?"

"I *tried* to, honey darling. I *tried* to. But nobody would
listen to me. Those girls were doin' naked dances on an
elevated stand in the center of the floor. Every Downtowner

there was eggin' 'em on! You should've seen Judge Moore and Hubert Erickson. And you should've heard that meek little hypocrite, Jerry Fant, yellin', 'More! More!' Shootin' craps is one thing. Naked women is another. I'm an ex-Downtowner from this minute. For two cents I'd tear the Dance Pavilion down after what's happened there tonight!''

He didn't go that far. It took more than naked women to turn him against his Dance Pavilion. However, he did begin to screen organizations that wanted to use it. From that day on, the Dance Pavilion was lent only to groups like the Ministerial Alliance, the W.C.T.U., the B'nai B'rith, the Boy Scouts, and the Eastern Star.

When Papa did tear the Dance Pavilion down, fifteen years later, he had a reason. None of his children had to ask him why because we knew. Parties weren't any fun for him any more without Mama. All you can see today—and you have to look hard—are a few of the stone pillars, almost obscured by weeds. The famous barbecue pit is there still, rusted and in ruins. The rest is gone. But the memories of schoolteachers eating barbecue, Ernie drinking beer, and the Downtowners encouraging their naked ladies remain.

A few yards from the Dance Pavilion, situated on a quiet little dirt road leading to the highway, was Papa's tourist court. Built long before the word "motel" was coined, these cottages of Papa's caught the eye of the tourist. Ernie Cooper had built them from his loveliest quarried sandstone. Their gabled roofs were covered with bright green shingles. Each cabin contained two bedrooms, a kitchenette, a bath, and a back porch. True, the bath wasn't tiled, the kitchenette wasn't equipped, and the beds sagged. Still, Papa could proudly proclaim (and he did): "There's not another tourist court in the whole U.S.A. with a wood-burnin' fireplace in every unit!"

The tourist court surprised everybody, including Papa, by turning out to be a good investment. During World War II all six houses were rented by the month to workers of the Douglas plant in Tulsa. Papa preferred "family people" to overnight trade. He lacked the temperament of an innkeeper. He worried too much about people's morals, motives, and emotions. "I can't stop thinkin' about what's goin' on in each one of 'em," he admitted.

The tourist court was not rented during one of my summer vacations from college. I wanted to run it to make some money. My brother was defying the Depression with his operation of the tavern on a snob basis. Up and down the road in both directions he placed signs saying: WELCOME HARVARD, WELCOME YALE, WELCOME DARTMOUTH, and WELCOME PRINCETON. He figured that if anyone in America had any money left to spend, it would be an alumnus of one of these Eastern schools who was driving through Oklahoma. He was right. Ivy Leaguers saw the signs and stopped for food. He even extended his sign campaign to include WELCOME WILLIAMS, WELCOME NOTRE DAME, and WELCOME BIG TEN.

The snob approach worked in the tavern, but it wouldn't work in the tourist court. You couldn't expect a snob to pay his money to sleep on one of those dreadful mattresses.

So I decided to charge bargain rates and settle for the common people.

Papa was opposed to my running the tourist court. He tried every way he could to discourage me.

"I know the score, Papa," I assured him. "I'm in college, remember?"

Papa wasn't sold on the idea yet. "I know you can do it, Sonny, but I ain't so sure I want you to do it. Y'see, many people who want to stay in the tourist court aren't really tourists. I mean—well, you've gotta take the bitter with the sweet, and—" He could see that being delicate was getting him nowhere. He decided to lay the cards on the table.

"*Pull up a chair and sit down!*"

I pulled up a chair and sat down.

"Now, Son, I'm gonna let you run the tourist court this summer because your brother has the tavern and you can use some money, too. But somebody's gotta tell you what you have to know, so it might as well be your old Dad. Rule One: *Always* have plenty of hot water."

"But Papa! When it's a hundred degrees outside, a person doesn't—"

"In *college*, huh? Do as I say. Always have hot water. You'll lose half your customers if you don't have it."

Now that he was launched, Papa threw himself wholeheartedly into his indoctrination course. "Rule Two: Some people get tired drivin' and want to rent a cabin for maybe just an hour or two to get a little rest. Don't look at 'em like you don't believe 'em. Keep still and mind your own business.

"Rule Three: Some of the people who look the tiredest from drivin' will have license plates from our own county. If they pay in advance, you've gotta believe 'em when they say they're tired!

"Rule Four: When ten couples in a row register as 'Mr. and Mrs. John Smith,' don't make any wisecracks. It's a very common name.

"Rule Five: Nobody ever got into trouble by keepin' his mouth shut."

He took a deep breath.

"Sonny boy, it's a degradin' kinda business. Bein' exposed to it can make you tough if you're not strong. But I know my son! You're gonna see what's wrong and you're gonna know what's right and you're not gonna let the wrong kinda people influence your life!"

That was as close as Papa ever came to telling me the Facts of Life. I soon found that with a tourist court I didn't need any further instruction.

Completing the cluster of buildings at the tourist stop was Papa's filling station. There were six pumps, an inordinate number in those days even by city standards. "A motorist in a hurry doesn't want to wait," Papa explained.

Inside the station was a natural-stone-walled, natural-stone-floored combination office and store (with a wood-burning fireplace). Behind this room were a living room, a kitchen, and a staircase leading to the second floor where there were two bedrooms. Ernie Cooper had faced the entire station with natural stone, unchiseled. The contrasting dark and light browns of the rock shapes were beautiful.

Papa was the station's best customer. His cars, trucks, tractors, and engines were always thirsty for gasoline. He took the rent out in trade and always owed a large balance after the rent was subtracted. Other customers, alas, were few and far between. Thousands of cars whizzed past every day but few stopped for gas. However, the filling station was a nice place for a man and his family to live—cool in the summer, cozy in the winter, with plenty of garden space, a lake to fish in, and a school bus stop at the front door.

It was when Papa decided to build a "twin" station across the road that all hell broke loose. The Depression was at its worst. Money for construction was nonexistent. But his building appetite craved nourishment.

When a bulldozer started scooping tons and tons of dirt out of the hill directly across from the filling station, people concluded that Papa was just clearing space for cars to pull off the highway before crossing over to get gas. When wagonloads of Ernie's choice rock were deposited in the cleared space, it was apparent that Papa had the building bug again.

Mama was the first to know about the new filling station.

"Annie," Papa began, "I guess you know how broke I am."

Mama was making a cake. "Everybody's broke," she said reassuringly.

"But I need two thousand dollars," Papa sighed. "I

want to build a station over there where I scooped out the hill." He stopped. "I won't build it if you tell me not to."

Mama looked up from her cake batter. "Did I ever tell you not to build anything, Max? That's your department. If you want to build a filling station, for heaven's sakes build it."

"But—well, I was wonderin' if you'd mind writin' your brother Ed to send you money from your part of the Levy estate. You could lend it to me, and—"

Mama set the bowl of cake batter on the sink, wiped her hands on her apron, walked over to Papa, and kissed him impulsively.

"Don't talk like that," she said softly. "You can't borrow anything from me, Max, because I already owe you more than I could ever pay back!"

Papa couldn't speak. He became inarticulate whenever he was touched. All he could do was look at Mama adoringly.

"I'll write Ed tonight," she said, putting the cake into the oven. "If the money's there, I'll get it."

Two days later Ed Levy arrived in person.

From the moment he stepped off the train, all through breakfast, all morning long, Ed sang the blues about money. The Levy Store was losing money every day. The Levy bank stock had not been paying dividends. Mesquite was taking the Levy lands. Ed went for a long walk on the ranch with Papa, complaining all the time.

After their return, Mama joined them on the front

porch. She knew her brother was giving Papa a bad time and she hoped to serve as moral support for the home team.

"Max," Ed began, "everything you've built on this place is a liability. A dozen cows in a barn built to hold two hundred. A chicken house without a chicken. All those tourist places empty. And that filling station over there—"

He didn't finish the sentence. As he looked at the filling station he saw a truck pull over to the scooped out side of the hill, deposit two huge storage tanks and six new gasoline pumps, and drive away.

Papa jumped up from his chair to escape.

"Max!" Uncle Ed barked. "Come back here! What are those pumps for?"

"What pumps?" Papa asked, looking toward the nursery.

"Those pumps over *there*," Ed said, pointing dramatically at the newly unloaded fixtures.

"Pumps?" Papa repeated. "Can't see why anyone would get so excited over a pump. If you folks will excuse me, I'll—"

"Max," Ed interrupted, purpling slightly. "You told me this morning that that filling station over there doesn't sell enough gasoline to support one family. Are you planning to build a *second* station?"

"Take it easy, Ed," Papa said softly. "It's not good for the blood pressure to get so excited in this hot weather."

"Don't change the subject!" Ed screamed. "Six pumps on one side! Six pumps on the other! Twelve pumps! That's eleven too many out here in the sticks!"

Papa looked at him, and said slowly, "Too *few*—or too many?"

"Don't *confuse* me, Max!" Ed steamed. He turned to Mama. "Annie, can't you make him listen to reason? He wants that two thousand dollars to build another *filling station!* Tell him two thousand dollars is like ten thousand dollars in these times."

Mama rested her head on the back of the swing, closed her eyes, and swung slowly.

"Justify yourself," Ed challenged Papa. "Just give me one reason why you want to squander two thousand on a second filling station when the first one's a failure."

Papa looked at Uncle Ed pityingly. All Ed knew was figures. He had no vision. He got no fun out of life. Patiently, as one teaches a slow child to read, Papa said, "Twin stations . . ." He paused to savor the lovely sound of those two words. "Twin stations will sell gas to cars on *both* sides of the highway. That's what's been wrong, Ed. I've only been gettin' 'em comin'. Now I'll get 'em comin' and *goin'!*"

Before Ed could answer, Mama stopped swinging, opened her eyes, and said brightly, "Heavens! It's after twelve o'clock. I'll bet you're both starved. Come inside. It's time for dinner."

Ed left for Texas that same night. When he got home he wrote Mama a letter which he had composed on the train. "Annie," it began, "you're married to a drunkard. Max is just as much a drunkard as a drunken bum in the gutter. He's a building drunkard. That quarry full of stones is his liquor supply. Ernie Cooper is his bartender. He mixes the drinks with mortar and cement. And Levy money pays for the toots. Enclosed is the check."

Ed got the last word. Papa got the filling station.

Compulsive builders like Papa have always been misunderstood by shortsighted people whose horizons are no farther away than the edges of a profit and loss sheet.

When Cheops insisted on building his pyramid he ran into opposition, too. He knew what he wanted, though. He was strong-willed. He got it. Papa and Cheops had a lot in common. Instead of building a great pyramid, Papa built three red hollow-tile silos. Since he had never had a silage problem on the ranch, one might argue that none of the silos was necessary. And certainly one would have been enough. Papa thought in terms of three, and he wouldn't settle for less. The three silos formed an equilateral triangle behind the barn. They towered imposingly over the entire ranch. They added dignity and beauty to the landscape. "They just *make* the place," Papa said, and he loved them.

When he built the silos, Papa had envisioned hundreds of cows enjoying the delicious silage he had stored up for them. It didn't work out that way. Not a single one of the silos was ever even partially filled. There were bugs which had to be ironed out. Surely Cheops had had to contend with bugs in his pyramid-building.

But there was another, even more basic problem. In desperation, Papa asked Dr. Fred Spencer of A and M College to come over and take a look at his silos.

Dr. Spencer toured the barn, inspected the impressive facilities for a large dairy herd, and then stood, lost in contemplation, before the three silos.

"They certainly are pretty," he said finally.

Papa beamed.

"And they are just like new," Dr. Spencer continued.

Papa explained the situation. "We haven't been storin' grain in 'em—because, well, to tell you the truth, Dr. Spencer, we don't know how in the hell to get the grain *inside*. We can't fill 'em from the bottom, and we don't know how to fill 'em from the top!"

Dr. Spencer nodded. "You've built them so tall that it's going to take tremendous power to send the grain through a chute to the top of the silo where it can drop in. Once it's in, you're O.K. You can take the silage out of the silo from the bottom through the openings along the side. Yes, all you need is power."

Papa thanked him for his advice and started thinking in terms of Power. Meanwhile we children spent hour after delirious hour climbing the stepladder rungs of the silos, sticking our heads inside the scary, hollow things, and getting echoes back that made our ears ring. I was one of the most popular boys in the sixth grade thanks to Papa's wonderful silos.

Papa got his power. I remember the day well because it was my birthday, June 22. After the ice cream and cake, Mama, my sisters, my brother, some school chums, and I were gathered on the front porch of the Big House drinking lemonade when the Power appeared. We missed Papa at the party. No one had the slightest idea where he was.

We'd called his usual haunts: the Farmer's Exchange, the post office, and Martin's Garage. Nobody had seen him.

One of my friends shouted suddenly, in a peculiar voice, "Look!"

We looked in the direction where he was staring.

About a mile up the highway a strange machine was coming toward us. As it neared the ranch it turned out to be a steam locomotive—a real one. Apart from the huge, wide steel wheels which had been added to it, it was a locomotive in every particular, from the engineer's booth to the steam whistle that toot-tooted its approach.

Everyone crowded to the porch railings. Some of the children waved and yelled at the strange thing which, to our amazement, stopped journeying down Highway 66 and turned into our own driveway, chugging straight toward the house.

"My God! It's your father!" Mama said, turning white.

Sure enough, there was Papa in the driver's seat of the locomotive, with Ernie Cooper as his fireman. Papa kept tooting the whistle as the frightening thing huffed and puffed down the drive. "Happy birthday, Sonny boy!" Then he sped down the driveway, cut across the back yard, and continued dizzily past the barn. With a tremendous screeching and popping and exploding and sizzling the locomotive settled to a stop at the foot of one of the silos.

By this time all of the spectators had run down to the silo to see the newest addition to the ranch. All except Mama. She stayed on the front porch, swinging slowly on the swing. One of my sisters had to fetch her a spot of bourbon, neat.

"How's this for a birthday present!" Papa shouted, pulling me up to the driver's seat of the quivering steam engine.

"Wonderful," I gasped, grabbing the cord and pulling several quick steam blasts. Never before, never since, had there been nor will there be a birthday present to equal Papa's locomotive.

Now that he had his Power, Papa built a long chute to feed the silage into the silo from the top. It worked—to a degree. It took quite a staff to man the locomotive, build up the steam power, and feed the grain into the chute. The Power shot the grain up high, all right, but unfortunately as much grain blew over the top and out of the silo as went inside. Horses, cows, and people sneezed for days after a session between the locomotive and the silos.

Finally Papa called it quits. The three silos remained virginal. They are still "like new" today. Papa will tell you, "All of the airlines route their planes over my ranch and sight on my three red silos. Wouldn't you say they're worth *something?*"

How he got the locomotive, where he got it, and what he paid for it will always remain a mystery. It stayed in that one spot for years, rusting away. Ultimately it became shells to bombard the Japanese in World War II. The locomotive was just one of Papa's plans that didn't work out. Read your history books! Things didn't always go perfectly for Cheops, either.

8. PAPA'S PRIVATE BASEMENT

There were some things you wouldn't have expected to find in Papa's basement—a white bearskin rug, for instance. There were no Picasso originals nor first editions of Shakespeare. There wasn't an electric typewriter nor a Stauffer reducing machine. But everything else was there: a weight-lifting machine, a penny scales, a pool table, a slot machine, twenty gasoline lanterns, a dressmaker's dummy, an eight-burner gas range, a twelve-compartment steam table, a 1932 Electrolux refrigerator, a row of showers along one wall, a bathroom (enclosed), two bathrooms (complete with fixtures but not enclosed). There were seven cots, four fanback wicker chairs, and eight desks. There were seventeen round-top dining tables. There was the largest fireplace in Oklahoma. There was a collection of bottles, labels, and a bottle-capping machine alongside the vat used for cooking Max Meyer's Famous Hot

Sauce. Hundreds . . . thousands . . . of things were there—somewhere.

You couldn't say that Papa saved everything. He didn't save pictures of movie stars, nor opium pipes, nor prayer rugs, nor kettledrums. He did save fire insurance policies on buildings long since sold or demolished, letters of application answering an ad for a nurseryman placed twenty-five years ago, old tennis balls, old checkerboards, bridles and bits, telephone books from every city in the country for the past fifty years, old calendars, canceled checks from banks long extinct. He saved every schoolbook of every child, beginning with the primers and continuing through high-school chemistry. He saved the first shoes of each child, velvet hats with white ribbons he'd bought for the girls at Marshall Field's, and Justin cowboy boots he'd commissioned for the boys. Framed, filed, or boxed was every diploma, honor scroll, prize award, citation, ribbon, pin, and medal belonging to his children. Every report card of every child from kindergarten through graduate school was in that basement.

It took very little searching to find children's furniture, Erector sets, fruit jars, Edison phonograph records, and croquet equipment. And pictures! *Pictures!* Albums with thousands of snapshots were double- and triple-decked on shelves. Hundreds of framed photographs, some enlarged out of proportion, and ranging in subject matter from Beatrice (aged four) and Pearl (aged two) doing a George and Martha Washington dance (in costume, yet) to the boys driving a goat cart, to the neighborhood small fry standing in a soggy row in borrowed bathing suits (one of the girls in this picture—the one earnestly picking her nose—later became a governor's wife), to pictures of the old store sign reading MAX MEYER, OUTFITTER TO MANKIND, to framed likenesses of all the relatives from Papa's side and one on Mama's (her father).

The seventeen round-top dining tables were stacked to the ceiling in a corner of the basement. Papa bought them for only fifty cents apiece and gave them away as fast as he was able. Many a guest has driven home from the ranch with one of Papa's tables in the trunk of his car. People cut them down for coffee tables or used them as they were for poker tables and patio tables. Some of Papa's tables were made from fine woods—walnut, cherry, mahogany. Papa, who never let style interfere with his sense of aesthetics, couldn't get over anyone's wanting to give them away because they were considered old-fashioned. He didn't use them himself because he needed more table room than they afforded. His master desk was the pool table, whose surface provided plenty of space for nursery catalogues, grandchildren's watercolors, blueprints for future construction jobs, newspaper clippings, other people's letters he had unsealed and must seal again, and roofing samples.

Papa's basement was wondrously cool. On hot days he'd strip down to his size-54 BVD's and roam barefoot on the cement floor, filing away new things and sorting out old ones. Once he found a seamstress who created for him vast, billowing tent-nightgowns, generously cut and slit up the sides for unchafed freedom. After his marriage to Jeanette he started wearing boxer shorts.

Papa emerged from his subterranean domain for meals

and phone calls. Then back to the basement he went for conferences with his crew, for mail answering, for the steaming of letters, and for the planning of campaigns of staggering significance.

Somewhere within this vast and wonderful basement was Papa's "steam room" where he censored all incoming mail. How he did it was his own secret. Did he have more equipment than the proverbial tea kettle? How did he prevent ink from smudging? How did he reglue letters without a crease or wrinkle?

Every member of our family was aware that Papa read all our mail first. My sisters told their boy friends, and my brother and I told our girl friends. Mama told her Texas kinfolks. If privacy was desired it had to be secured through a long-distance telephone call (when Papa wasn't near an extension) or by addressing mail to general delivery. Papa had peeking privileges to all mail that came to the house and to the family post-office box. He steamed all letters open, read them, and resealed them. Letters marked "personal" got priority.

Papa would hand us our mail, pre-perused. We knew he had tampered with it, and he knew we knew it, so why discuss it? It wasn't censorship in the technical sense because Papa never deleted anything nor held a letter back nor lectured anyone about a letter's contents. He might have been tempted, but he never did it.

When I was in law school I fell hard for a girl from Cleveland who always smelled of Coty's L'Aimant and whose letters were doused in that intrusive fragrance. She was petite and so was her handwriting. In fact, she prided herself on a minuscule script which was perfectly formed but which required a magnifying glass for comfortable deciphering. Without a word's being said, I knew Papa was getting a huge kick out of her letters to me. One day when he handed me my perfumed bit of fine print, I looked up and said casually, "Tell me what she says, Papa. I'll never be able to read it in this light."

Papa assumed a look of injured innocence and started to protest until his sense of humor got the best of him. His hurt look changed into a slowly expanding grin. He leaned over my shoulder and whispered confidentially, "You're right, Sonny boy. Tell her to start writin' bigger or she's gonna ruin our eyes!"

If one of us did succeed in circumventing Papa's OSS techniques it was a known fact that unless the letter was torn into bits and flushed down the toilet, Papa would learn its contents eventually. There was no hiding place he couldn't ferret out. So we accepted Papa's steaming as graciously as we could, and pretended it didn't exist.

It would look better if one could say that Papa's letter steaming was restricted to members of his own family. But his silent censoring embraced all whose letters came under his jurisdiction. Relatives never dreamed that Papa knew the scuttlebutt from home before they did, and more than one visitor was shocked speechless by Papa's psychic powers.

Papa not only read our mail before we opened it. He also filed it away for future reference after we had answered it. In his basement he had box after box of letters—from old sweethearts, friends, classmates, employers, and creditors.

One day last summer when I was out at the ranch, Papa walked upstairs to the kitchen door, stuck his head out to call to me, and returned to his lower kingdom. I answered his summons immediately. I was struck with the coolness of the basement and the half-light. Papa was barefoot as usual and wore candy-striped boxer shorts. I expected him to show me a blueprint for some new structure, or to ask my advice on the wording of an ad for a nurseryman or dairyman or ranch foreman. Instead, Papa invited me to sit down in one of the fanback chairs and relax. He disappeared into a far corner of the basement for a minute and returned with a bundle of letters, neatly tied with a thick rubber band. He held them out to me with a very solemn look. I took them and glanced down at the top letter. When I saw the microscopic handwriting my mouth popped open and wouldn't close.

"Good golly, Papa," I finally sputtered. "You don't mean you've saved those letters all these years!"

"They're all here in order," he said. "From first to last."

"Did you save *all* our love letters?"

"Yep," Papa said. "And some of 'em would make your sisters squirm if they could see 'em now. If I let their *husbands* see 'em, there'd be a riot!"

I got a strange feeling when I thought of my wife reading my old letters—and (it was merely a matter of time) my children getting a charge out of them! This thought had occurred to Papa. "Sonny," he said, "I asked you down here to the basement today to give you these letters. If something happened to me and someone found them here, it might be kinda embarrassin' for you."

"That's putting it mildly," I said, walking over to the mammoth fireplace and squatting on the hearth. "Mind if I burn them here?"

"Why not?" Papa said.

I took some book matches from my pocket and hesitated a second before striking one. I lifted the stack of letters to my nose and whiffed.

"The smell's gone," I said.

Papa nodded.

"Wonder whatever happened to her?" I said, as the flames from one old letter consumed another—from first to last.

"I don't know," Papa answered softly. "But wherever she is, I hope she learned how to use a typewriter."

Papa's filing technique was superb. He could put his finger on anything about anybody at any time. On the thirtieth anniversary of my graduation from Sapulpa High School Papa mailed copies of the *Sapulpa Herald* containing my picture and graduation speech to my wife, my in-laws, and several of my clients. He not only saved clippings about members of his own family but about friends and neighbors, too. An old classmate, now a famous surgeon at Johns Hopkins, wrote me a letter recently telling me how flabbergasted he had been at receiving from my father a newspaper story of his victory in an oratorical contest when he was a sophomore in high school. The clipping was thirty-two years old.

On another day at the ranch, as I started to leave, I discovered a wad of papers in my coat pocket.

"What in the world are these?" I asked.

"Oh, just some things you've forgotten about," Papa said. "Read 'em later."

I glanced at the collection: a theme I'd written in eighth grade entitled "The Evils of Alcohol," a picture of my second-grade class at Washington School, a write-up of the first oil well in the Max Meyer Addition to Kellyville. There were many others—yellowed with age, but intact.

"I'll take them with me on the plane tomorrow, Papa. I'm going to Dallas on business."

He was aching to ask what the business was about but figured he'd find out eventually. "Goin' to Taro to see the Levys?"

"I probably won't have time. It's a quick trip."

"Well, if you do see 'em, give 'em my love," Papa said, scratching himself.

I said I would.

"And bring me a new Dallas telephone directory. The one I've got now is ten years old."

I had somehow got the job of keeping Papa supplied with telephone directories.

"How many phone books do you have, Papa?"

"About seventy-five. Everybody in Sapulpa knows I collect 'em. People call here all the time for addresses of folks in other cities."

"Everybody in Sapulpa knows that you collect *everything*," I laughed. "Some of those pictures and newspaper clippings of yours must go back fifty years."

"Sixty! Sixty-five!" Papa corrected. "Someplace in the

basement I've got an old Taro paper with an article about your grandfather's opera house. It's dated 1897."

"You've got a filing system like a newspaper morgue," I said.

"Like a *what?*" Papa asked, certain he'd misunderstood.

"A morgue. That's what they call it at the paper. The Morgue—the place where they save all the clippings and pictures and information about people."

Papa spat. "Son," he said sternly. "I'm surprised at you! That's a *terrible* word and I don't like it." He spat again. "That . . . uh . . . word means death. All my clippings— even the real old ones—are alive. That's what makes 'em so nice to look at over and over." He spat a third time. "Have a nice trip to Texas," he said, kissing me as he always did when a child went away. "And don't ever use that awful word again."

I'm sure he spat seven times over his left shoulder the minute my car was out of sight.

When Papa cooked in his basement it was a production to dwarf the most extravagant of TV spectaculars. He stripped down to his BVD's, or tent-gown, or boxer shorts, and barred everybody except Ernie Cooper, his chief barbecuer. The two of them engaged in the mysterious rite of hot-sauce cookery as it has never been practiced before or since.

Papa grew all of the ingredients in his own garden. Into the gurgling cauldron he'd dump tomatoes, onions, sweet peppers, green peppers, hot peppers, very hot peppers, and very red-hot peppers. It was the hottest hot sauce in history. It was volcanic, lethal, dangerous. Yet everyone who tasted it begged for some to take home. Papa passed it out in half pints. A half pint of his sauce, properly diluted with ketchup, made at least a half gallon of barbecue sauce. The ratio was roughly eight parts ketchup to one part hot sauce. Anyone who tried to use it straight needed plastic surgery on the roof of his mouth after the first swallow. Papa's hot sauce was wonderful on meat, in soups, in salad dressings, on scrambled eggs, and as a general seasoning. Papa's friend Judge Wright said once, "Max Meyer's hot sauce? It's a way of life!"

When the manager of the local Safeway Store requested several bottles of the stuff to sell in the store, Papa got excited. He envisioned himself as a barbecue sauce tycoon with millions of dollars flowing in from his atomic mixture. He immediately had ten thousand labels printed:

MAX MEYER'S FAMOUS HOT SAUCE

Grown and Bottled on the

MAX MEYER RANCH

5 Miles West of Sapulpa, Okla., U.S.A.

He delivered three dozen half pints, properly labeled, and waited for reorders.

A week later Papa got a phone call from the Safeway manager who was about to strangle from excitement. "My God, Max! What in the hell's *in* that hot sauce?"

"Why?"

"*Why?* Last night five of the bottles exploded. You

oughta *see* this mess! Hot sauce and glass all over the store—from soups to soaps. I've had three calls from customers saying that theirs exploded at home. They're all as mad as hornets. I'm going to throw the rest of this TNT away!"

"Don't you *dare!*" Papa yelled. "I'll drive into town right now and pick it up."

While Papa was on his way to reclaim his sauce, the manager took no more chances. He uncapped the few remaining bottles as gingerly as a weapon detonator handles a hot bomb.

After that Papa just gave the hot sauce away as a gift to his friends, warning them to keep it uncorked and in the refrigerator. "Better add a little ketchup to it," he'd suggest as an afterthought. If the recipient would ask naively, "How much?", Papa'd grin and say, "About six times as much as you think you oughta!"

Papa did most of his thinking in his basement. He made all of his major decisions there. I was a party to one of them.

It was a drizzly, gray Thanksgiving Day on the ranch in 1946. Papa had called us all together—Bea, Harold, and their children from St. Louis; Pearl, Stanley, and their sons; my brother, Manny, who was in the regular army; and me.

The Big House was warm and pleasant. Papa had wood fires blazing in the living room and the upstairs bedroom. He'd had someone come in to clean the place from top to bottom so the girls wouldn't find fault with his housekeeping.

The Thanksgiving dinner was the kind Mama used to prepare for us: Turkey, corn bread dressing, cranberries, sweet potatoes, and pumpkin pie. There was too much of everything. I knew that each of us was remembering Mama through the dinner. No one spoke her name, but she was in everybody's eyes and heart. We half expected her to walk back into the room from the kitchen bringing something more for us to eat. She had died suddenly of a stroke, in 1940, leaving Papa, who was sixty years old, bewildered and forlorn. None of us could get used to the idea that she was gone for good.

After dinner, the grandchildren put on layers of clothing and hiked to the lake. Bea, Pearl, Harold, and Stanley started a bridge game. I was deciding whether to curl up on the couch with, or without, a newspaper when Papa pulled at my sleeve and said quietly, "Follow me, Son."

He led the way to the basement—a place none of us ventured into any more without an invitation. It hadn't occurred to me that the mammoth fireplace here would be going full force until I saw it. I stood by it for a minute or two, hypnotized by the flames. Papa called me out of my reverie and motioned me to a chair near one of his desks. He opened one of the desk drawers and brought out some letters.

I squirmed. Papa was going to confront me with evidence of another of my red-hot correspondences which had fizzled out. I was trying to figure out who used to write to me on blue stationery when Papa said, "Son, these letters are all mine. If I asked you to read just one of 'em—as a personal favor to your Dad—would you do it?"

Letters to Papa! Love letters he hadn't had to steam open or reseal!

"Of course, Papa. Let me see one."

Reluctantly, shyly, he handed me the letter on top. "My dear Max," it began. It spoke freely about the weather, mutual friends, personal things. It was signed, "With love, Jeanette."

I looked up. Now it was Papa's turn to stare into the fire. His tanned cheeks glowed red in the reflection of the flames. Or was he blushing? He seemed to be looking into the fire for something he had lost there. He turned his head to me and said slowly, "Sonny boy, the Big House is full of racket today with the kids runnin' around and all. Tomorrow it'll be the way it was yesterday and the way it is every other day—quiet as hell. You children keep busy. Bea and Pearl have their own homes. Your brother has his army job. You have your own apartment now. I . . . well, I'm just all by myself in this big old place."

I started to apologize for moving out to a place of my own, but Papa wouldn't let me.

"You can't stay cooped up with your Dad all your life, Son. You did the right thing in gettin' yourself an apartment. You've gotta be with young people your own age. You've gotta start thinkin' about gettin' a family of your own."

I looked around Papa's basement. Shadows from the fireplace stippled the walls. The slate sky sent cold gray streaks into the corners where the fire didn't reach.

"You're lonely, Papa."

Papa kept looking into the fire.

"And you've . . . found somebody?"

He turned to me and pointed to the letter I was holding. "Y'see, Son, it's this way. Aunt Molly Goldstein out in California knew this lady. She got us started writin' to each other. We've been correspondin' for quite a spell." He gestured at the stack of letters. "I haven't told anyone about it except you. The others won't understand at first. They may think I mean a disrespect to your mother. I—"

This was my moment of closeness with my father. Without his saying so, I saw how selfish we children had been in our attitudes toward him. In the six years since Mama had died we had gone to new things ourselves, yet we had expected Papa to be exactly the same as he had been when Mama was alive. I saw now how impossible this was. Papa couldn't live alone. He needed an audience, and he was wasting away for the lack of one. He was trying to tell me that he wanted to marry again. But he had to take the long way round. Too *long*—or too *short?*

"Papa," I said, "I'm going to tell you what people are always telling me: 'It is better to marry than to burn.' That's from the Bible."

"There are lots of ways to burn," Papa said. "I'm past the bonfire stage, Son. I'd just like a little kindlin'—enough to take the damp out of a cold house."

He folded the blue paper back into the envelope, replaced the letter, and put his correspondence back into the desk drawer.

"Am I makin' a mistake, Son?"

If I'd said, "Yes," he'd have backed out. It was that close a decision.

"Papa! Have you forgotten what you always told us when we were afraid of making mistakes? You said, 'Remember Davy Crockett! Be sure you're right. Then go ahead!' You're sure about Jeanette . . . aren't you?"

"I . . . think so."

"Then go ahead! If the others squawk, leave 'em to me."

I think that was what Papa wanted to hear me say. He stood up, grinned, and said, "Let's go upstairs and finish that 'punkin' pie."

9. PROJECT TRENCH

Papa had as much fun tearing down as he had building up. This fun was his, "all expenses paid," when the State of Oklahoma widened Highway 66.

It was February, 1952. The thermometer registered ninety-five degrees. Each year this "false spring" comes to Oklahoma, almost to the day. It's not unusual for flowers to bloom and fruit trees to blossom. Then a hard freeze or heavy snow follows within a matter of hours.

The adjuster for the State was obviously under a strain as he sat on the natural-stone back porch fanning himself. All 126 casement windows were closed.

"Mr. Meyer, I really hate to have to tell you this but . . . well, your filling station has been condemned by the Highway Department for the widening project."

Papa showed no emotion. "Which station?" he asked softly.

159

"Why, the one alongside the hill."

Papa could hardly believe what he was hearing. This second station, which his brother-in-law had hexed from the start, was a financial failure. Instead of cars pulling in to fill up with gasoline at its tanks, they persisted in crossing the road and trading with the larger, original station near the tavern and tourist court. Since Papa had built the second station solely to catch this other-side-of-the-road trade, the motorists' refusal to co-operate infuriated him. The second station, with its green gabled roof and its natural-stone exterior, was little more than window dressing. It didn't pay to keep gasoline in the tanks. And now this man from the State had come to ask permission to tear it down. Papa found it difficult to control himself.

"I love that station," Papa said. "It's my favorite building on the ranch. I scooped out a whole section of the hill to build it there. Are you *sure* you have to destroy it?"

"Yes, Mr. Meyer. The new road will run right through the middle of the station. It will have to be demolished. Of course, you'll be compensated."

Papa excused himself. He walked into the kitchen where Jeanette, his new wife, was washing dishes. "Jeanette, would you be good enough to make a big pitcher of lemonade?"

"Why, sure, Max." She looked at him. "You look pale. Are you feeling sick?"

"Oh, I feel fine. Fine. Maybe you could find some cookies someplace to serve with the lemonade?"

Jeanette made the lemonade, filled a plate with cookies,

and brought them to the porch in time to hear Papa say, "Eight thousand dollars? Why, you couldn't *begin* to replace that beautiful filling station for eight thousand dollars! And it's an income producer, too. Doesn't the State take that into consideration?"

"But Mr. Meyer, it isn't being used now, is it?"

"No-o-o, not at present. I'm working on a deal with an oil company to lease both stations to 'em. If they can get only one, the whole deal may fall through. Twelve thousand."

The adjuster drank half his lemonade, ate two cookies, and said, "Ten."

Ten thousand dollars for the station which he'd built for two! Papa kept his poker face. "Well, you're gettin' the best of me, but I'll take ten thousand dollars for the station on one condition."

"What's that?"

"That you let me tear the station down and keep the materials."

"It's a deal," the adjuster said.

Papa spilled lemonade all over his shirt front.

The demolition of the filling station not only furnished Papa with the money he needed for several new projects, it enabled him to set up a kind of permanent construction gang which was always at his beck and call. Two Indians were permanent fixtures of this gang. Papa called one of them "Big Indian," the other one "Little Indian."

How he met up with the Indians is anyone's guess. He

probably knew their parents from the days when he had the store. His affinity for and understanding of the Indian temperament caused these young Indians to like him immediately.

There were three Indians in the beginning. Big Indian and Little Indian were brothers. The third Indian was a vague sort of younger cousin. Big Indian had a white wife, Little Indian had an Indian wife and baby, and the cousin was unmarried.

These three Indian boys were typical of many of their generation of full bloods in Oklahoma—neither compatible with the Supermarket Generation of white boys their age, nor any longer a part of the blanket-wearing, braided-hair world of their parents. They wore the dignity of their heritage gracefully, and they kept whatever feelings of resentment and frustration they might have solely to themselves. These Indians were so noncommunicative that Papa must have made his deal with them without words being spoken.

The Indians liked Papa's setup. He gave them, rent free, two of the nicer houses on what was left of his once flourishing housing project for unemployed families which he called WPA Row. The Little Indians took one of the houses. Mr. and Mrs. Big Indian and the cousin lived next door. Papa supplied water, electricity, gas, wood for the wood-burning fireplaces, beds, chairs, tables, a cow—which the wives took turns milking—a vegetable garden, fruit jars for canning, and Epsom salts at regular intervals.

All three of the Indians rarely worked at the same time.

One or two of them would go hunting, or fish in the lake, or disappear into town for a couple of days. There was always at least one of Papa's Indians on call, and when properly alerted, all three were available.

The married Indians liked this arrangement so much that they settled down permanently in the two houses. The third Indian eventually married a city girl who refused to live on the ranch. However, he drove his '48 Ford to the ranch every day to work—or to enjoy the silent company if there was no work to be done. He, too, was happy with this satisfactory sort of "reservation" which fitted the needs and yearnings of an unadjusted generation of a forgotten people.

Papa called the Indians his "crew." They would have qualified as his bodyguards if he had needed guarding. Papa took them with him when he drove to Tulsa for car parts from a salvage yard, when he drove to a nearby farm to carry roofing materials to a tenant, and when he went for groceries at the Farmer's Exchange.

It was a striking entourage. Papa, tall, gigantic, powerful, almost as brown as an Indian himself, leading the way, with his one, two, or three (as the case might be) Indians following after him, single file. The four of them shared their precious silence. The boys seldom spoke to each other, even in Indian. They rarely said anything to Papa. Papa, in the manner of an ancient chieftain, bargained and negotiated for them at the City Drug, the Farmer's Exchange, and J. C. Penney's, sparing them the indignity of talk.

It was Papa's task to think up jobs to keep his Indians busy. This was easy because the Indians themselves didn't care too much about consecutive employment. After the filling station was demolished, Papa planned the island in the lake. Then he would be ready to tackle the trench around the house. Then there was the never-ending chore of taking up old water lines that were rusted to pieces and replacing them with new ones. There was plenty to do, all right. Papa's problem was to maintain the proper balance between the doing of it and the affording of it.

The filling station was torn down as lovingly as it had been built. Papa directed his Indians to save all windows and doorframes, all beams and planks, and even all nails and spikes that could be used again. Most of the materials were stored in the basement of the Big House.

Some months later when the Indians started hauling away the filling station's old sandstone and stacking it neatly alongside the Big House it was apparent that the building bug had bitten Papa again.

"I need help," Jeanette confided to me on the telephone. "I'm afraid I don't understand what your father is going to do with all this stone. He couldn't possibly be thinking of *enlarging the house*, could he?"

"Where Papa's concerned, anything's possible," I answered her. "Maybe he's going to build another powder room."

"There's too much rock for that," Jeanette sighed. "Besides, he whistles and hums all the time the way he does when he's real happy. He wouldn't whistle and hum like that if he weren't going to build something *big*. Why don't all of you come to the ranch Sunday? Come in the morning and spend the whole day."

I had to wait until Sunday to learn about Project Trench.

It was a warm, cloudless spring day. The sky was a clear, light Oklahoma blue and there was no hint of trouble in the offing. I was married now and had two small daughters. We started for the ranch around ten o'clock. When we made the turn at the top of the hill and saw the flag flying on the flagpole, we knew that we were officially expected.

As I slowed down to make the left turn into the driveway, my children spotted Papa chatting with Ernie Cooper amid the ruins of the demolished filling station. We waved at him, then turned in at the Big House, followed the circle drive, and stopped under the porte-cochere.

Jeanette met us at the door. She wore an organdy apron and a worried look. "I haven't been able to find out a *thing*," she announced as soon as we were in the house.

She led the way to the huge back porch, opened one of the 126 casement windows, and pointed to the immense pile of rock that had been deposited near the house.

"He knows I'm dying of curiosity," Jeanette said. "Maybe he's just trying to tease me."

I shook my head. "You don't know Papa. When he starts moving rock, he means business."

We heard Papa come to the front part of the house and we broke up our parley. He was in wonderful spirits. He grabbed his granddaughters and lifted them, one under each arm, parading around with them as though they were sacks of sugar. They squealed their pleasure. Then he let the children down, patted my wife on the hand, kissed me, and led the way to the back porch where the table was set with his favorite Sunday menu: fried chicken, mashed potatoes and gravy, new peas, cranberries and hot rolls, with blackberry cobbler for dessert.

After the last bite of cobbler was finished, I led into the mystery of the rocks as casually as I could. "Papa, now that your filling station is torn down and the State has awarded you the money, I hope you'll take a good, long vacation."

"Yes," my wife said. "Now's the opportunity for you two to go to California and stay as long as you please."

"I'd like that," Jeanette said brightly. "I'd like to show Papa California. We've been married six years and he's never had a trip."

Papa ran his spoon round and round the empty cobbler dish. When he was satisfied that no cobbler remained, and that he was supposed to say something, he made his announcement.

"I can't afford to go to California this year," he said. "Maybe next year. Too much to do on the place now. *First* thing is to build the trench around the house. That's a three months' job."

Silence.

"The trench?" I asked.

"Yep. I've got to do something about the basement fillin' up with water. No point in completin' the rathskeller —*some* day—if there's gonna be water on the floor every time it rains."

"I can't see how a trench—" Jeanette began.

"I've talked with a dozen people," Papa said. "They all tell me I should build a ditch all the way around the foundation of this house. Then, after cementin' around the foundation, I should fill the ditch with rock and stone so's the water'll seep down it faster than it does anywhere else. Then I'll build a drainage canal to lead off the surplus water. Mark my word, three months from now the basement will be dry as a bone."

Jeanette looked relieved. The rock pile was accounted for. A ditch was much less of a threat to her housekeeping problems than a new wing to the house.

"Will you get some contractor to do the job?" I asked.

"I should say *not!*" Papa replied emphatically. "My crew can dig a ditch better than anybody! I know exactly how to build it. It's called a French drain. Come outside, Sonny boy, and I'll show you exactly what we're gonna do."

I walked around the house with Papa, but I knew no more after the tour was over than I did beforehand. I still do not understand the principle on which a French drain works. I wonder now whether Papa ever did, either.

For weeks, the Indians, under Papa's surveillance, worked on Project Trench. The ditch was deeper than I had thought it would be. They dug it flush to the Big House to the depth of the foundation itself. One Indian crushed rock and the other two dug. They took turns. Then, when the ditch was deep enough, Ernie Cooper stepped in, or rather, jumped down, and cemented along the bottom of the ditch to make the foundation watertight. Then the crushed rock was shoveled into the ditch and dirt packed onto the surface.

The near calamity occurred the day Ernie got the Indians drunk. The French drain had progressed almost all the way around the house and was complete except for the last link at the corner of the back porch. Papa had gone to town for cement.

Ernie had got hold of a pint of Three Feathers and offered the Indians a swig apiece to celebrate the completion of their trench. After they had killed Ernie's pint, the youngest Indian drove his '48 Ford to town and bought another pint from the bootlegger. The whisky stimulated the boys to dig deeper. Since the supply of crushed rock was adequate, all three got shovels and tried to see who could dig the fastest. Ernie spurred them on, yelling, "Dig, men! Dig till you strike oil an' get rich!"

The usually taciturn Indians became noisy and explosive. They dug the French drain deeper and deeper, angling it under the foundation of the house. From deep inside the trench they started shoveling dirt on each other, at first playfully, then in fury. Just as they started beating each other over the heads with their shovels, the foundation pillar supporting the corner of the house made a peculiar noise, as if it were going to buckle.

Jeanette was in the living room when she heard the creaking sound. She ran to the porch, took one look, dashed to the telephone, called Bailey Lumber, got Papa on the phone, shouted, "The house is falling in!" and hung up.

Papa drove the five miles from town in three minutes, turned into the driveway like a racing car, circled the house to the back of the drive, jumped out of the car before it had come to a stop, and started screaming at his crew, "Start shovelin'! Get out of that ditch and start shovelin'! Start pitchin' the dirt *back!*"

It was something to see. The Indians were so wobbly they could hardly climb out of the trench. Finally they made it, and slowly started shoveling dirt into the hole to fill it up. Papa grabbed a shovel, filled it with dirt, and threw the dirt into the trench smack onto Ernie Cooper, who had passed out down there. Ernie came to with a start, concluded that he was being buried alive, jumped out of the trench, and ran toward the lake screaming like a maniac.

Miraculously, the house didn't cave in. The original foundation withstood the concerted effort of all three people to undermine it. The sound that frightened Jeanette proved to be only a groan of warning. The dangerous ditch had been filled in the nick of time.

Papa punished his Indians by refusing for a whole week to take them into town with him.

That spring was one of the rainiest in the history of Oklahoma. The trench assumed the proportions of a king-sized irrigation ditch, brimming over with water. The terminus of the new drainage canal became a small pond in the front yard. The water stood six inches deep in the basement.

Seeing that the French drain didn't accomplish its purpose, Papa asked a building contractor to come out and take a look. It took him just two minutes to find the crack in the basement wall. He showed Papa how the water was seeping into the basement through this crack under the porch. It took Ernie thirty minutes and half a sack of cement to repair the leak.

Papa was right. By the end of his three-month time limit, the basement was dry as a bone.

10. PAPA AND THE HEALING ARTS

Papa had gas. It must have had something to do with his gall bladder, or with his fondness for raw vegetables. He spent a good deal of time standing in front of the vegetable bins at the Farmer's Exchange eating fresh garden peas, leaf lettuce, turnips, and snap beans by the fistful.

While Papa never discussed his condition, one had the feeling that he had tried to do something about it, had failed, and had resigned himself to it. "You have to be bloated yourself before you can understand what others go through," he said. "Havin' gas is like bein' bald. There's nothing you can do about it but live with it."

We lived with Papa's gas almost as easily as he did. We knew that he was as discreet as it was humanly possible to be, and we suffered with him when strangers caused him to repress and restrain his pressures to his discomfort and

171

embarrassment. Papa was a modest man. Modesty and gas are practically irreconcilable.

I was no more than eight or nine when we had house guests from Camden, New Jersey. The man's name was Moe. I forget Moe's wife's name. They had come to Camden, New Jersey, from Grandma Meyer's home town of Bialystok, in Poland, on tickets purchased with Papa's money through Grandma Meyer's above-water version of the Underground Railroad.

Moe and his wife were Papa's sixth cousins, once removed. At his mother's request, Papa had written them a letter of welcome when they first arrived in this country, adding, as he always did, "Come and see us whenever you're in Oklahoma, and stay as long as you please." They aimed for our house on Oak Street the minute they hit Sapulpa.

Moe and his wife originally announced their intention of staying only overnight on their way from Camden to Pasadena (with cousin-stops at Amarillo, Phoenix, and Bakersfield). A cloudburst forced them to stretch their impromptu visit to an extra day and night.

The next day was a wet, gloomy Sunday. Everybody was trapped indoors, including Moe and his wife. Papa, who could not stand being cooped up anywhere, began to stalk restlessly from room to room. If he looked over-stuffed after breakfast, by noon he was distended. The huge helpings of chicken, dressing, mashed potatoes, and peach cobbler he devoured at dinner didn't make his situation any less tense.

Papa repeatedly went to the front door and looked outside at Oak Street. When he discovered the rain coming down in bucketfuls, with no letup in sight, he looked miserable.

Some people can burp away discomfiture. Papa was not equipped with such flexible two-way plumbing. My father never burped nor belched, in private or in public. (I do not say this boastfully. It is not really a family trait to be proud of. As a matter of fact, there were certain other gastric noises, both in private and in public, which could have given a lifelong complex to a thinner-skinned relative.)

Papa made an effort at being hospitable. He sat down and visited with his cousins, only to jump up in alarm when his stomach started communicating ungodly gurglings and bubblings to the room at large.

We knew what Papa was suffering, and we ached for him. We also knew that, with company in the house, the bathroom was off limits. Stout walls and locked doors were no match for his perturbations. He was overly sensitive about being heard.

Finally, as the rain slackened momentarily from a torrent to a downpour, Papa made his decision. "Excuse me," he said suddenly, "I've gotta run to the garage to see if it's leakin'!"

Cousin Moe, unaware of a crisis, said affably, "Let it leak, Max. What can it hurt in the garage?"

"Yes," agreed Mrs. Moe. "What can it hurt?"

"It can . . . hurt . . . *plenty!*" Papa gasped, running for the door, bolting across the porch, and racing down the driveway.

"He'll get drenched," Moe's wife said helplessly. "He shouldn't run in the rain like that."

And then, before anyone could answer her, the first blast was heard. It came from halfway down the driveway. It was followed by three more abrupt reports, equally noisy. "What's that?" Moe asked uneasily. "Sounds like shots."

The next detonations were only slightly muffled. They came from the garage. There were many of them, each one sharp and clear. Moe's wife kept wanting to know what the sounds could be. Moe, by nature suspicious, had already decided that Papa's frequent trips to the front door had something to do with a secret enemy Papa was on the alert for. Now he was convinced that the enemy had sighted Papa and was shooting at him.

My mother, flushed with stifled laughter, mumbled something about "tidying things up a bit" and rushed from the living room toward the kitchen.

It was my sister Bea who showed real presence of mind. She went to the piano and began a loud rendition of the "Scarf Dance," so abandoned in its rhythm that the guests looked at her appalled.

With the sound of Papa's unmistakable step on the front porch, Bea stopped playing as unexpectedly as she had begun. She wheeled around on the piano stool to face him.

He was dripping wet. His hair was plastered down on his forehead. His shirt was soaked and clinging to his skin. But his face told a story of relaxation and relief. In place of the tenseness that had obsessed him, his old geniality had returned. "You were right, Moe," he said to his cousin.

"The garage is perfectly O.K. You folks excuse me for a minute and I'll change to some dry clothes. Go on, Beatrice darling, play your piece."

Bea swung herself around to the piano and played the "Scarf Dance" slowly and painfully from beginning to end. She used the soft pedal all the way.

Papa's ideas about medicines, diseases, and bodily disorders were unique. His beliefs blended the teachings of Mary Baker Eddy with the philosophy of Emile Coué. And there was a strong African witch-doctor influence thrown in for good measure. Papa didn't like to talk about illness. He didn't like to be told that people were sick. He must have felt that if one refused to recognize a cold, or an earache, or poison ivy, the malady would be insulted by the indifference and disappear.

When one of the children said, "Mama's sick. She has a bad headache," Papa immediately corrected him with, "Shhhhh. Mama's all right. She hasn't got a headache at all. Tell her to stop *thinkin'* about headaches. *You* stop thinkin' about 'em, too!" Then he'd run to Mama and say, "Annie darling, you haven't got a headache, *have* you? It's just the light affectin' your eyes." (Or the "old air" in the room, or "nervousness.") Papa often talked people out of seemingly valid complaints.

Contagious diseases made him mad. When my brother got the mumps we met Papa at the door of the sickroom and told him dramatically that Manny had the mumps and he'd better stay out.

"Stay *out?* Why should I stay *out?*" he wanted to know.

"Because mumps are *catching*," we said. "We've had them—but you haven't, so you've got to stay out."

"You're insane," Papa said, and walked in. He looked accusingly at Manny as if to say, "They've talked you into this." Then he leaned over and kissed the boy.

"Papa, you shouldn't kiss Manny," one of us protested. "You'll catch the mumps."

He faced us defiantly. "*What's* catchin'? He's my *own child*, isn't he? My own flesh and blood! Do you think he's going to make his own Dad sick?" Then, just to cinch his point, he kissed Manny again, on the lips. (Papa always kissed his children on the lips. When we were very young, and after we had children of our own, he still kissed the same way. There were times when I thought I'd die of embarrassment when huge, hulking Papa met me at the railroad station, bent down, and kissed me on the mouth in front of my college friends. I survived his unabashed affection and I'm glad I didn't complain.)

Papa believed that it was impossible to catch germs from someone younger than yourself. I heard him say this many times. Little children especially were incapable of transmitting germs. Once I caught Papa drinking what was left of a glass of water he had brought to his feverish granddaughter. I said, "You shouldn't drink after Elizabeth, Papa. She has a temperature and you'll get her germs."

He was most indignant. "*I* shouldn't drink after my own little granddaughter? *I* should be afraid to drink from the same glass that this sweet, pure, innocent baby of a darling girl has drunk from? You're crazy!"

Either Papa had had all the childhood diseases or he was immune to them. At any rate, he never caught mumps, measles, chicken pox, whooping cough, or any disease we children had—and we had them all. Perhaps his immunity was traceable to his defiance of the germ theory. It was impossible to "catch" a germ one walked away from!

When Papa ailed, he called it "a very slight touch of a cold." He was his own doctor. He stomped around the house, barefoot, wearing a tent of a nightgown and a wildly decorated purple woolen robe. He smeared his face and nose with Mentholatum, and he took Epsom salts. Then he drank copious quantities of hot lemonade tea, sweated, dried himself with a large bath towel, drank more tea, sweated some more, changed his nightgown, and announced to all of us that he was well already. He was, too.

Mentholatum . . . and Epsom salts! Some people recall a parent when they hear a song or see a flower or read something nostalgic. I think of my father whenever I see a Mentholatum ad or hear the word "Epsom." On my own, I have had enough Mentholatum stuffed up my nose to retire the bonded indebtedness of the Mentholatum company. Papa always bought the largest jars and tubes he could find. He would have purchased the stuff in vat lots if they'd sold it to him that way. Mentholatum, to Papa, was preventative as well as prescriptive. Even when one was feeling fine it was a good idea, he thought, to "stuff a little Mentholatum up your nose." If you had a sore throat Papa would butter a cloth with Mentholatum and pin the cloth around your neck for twenty-four hours. (Try this sometime for a new kind of touch sensation!)

Stuffing Mentholatum up our noses was a nightly ritual. We hated it. We submitted to it simply because Papa was so passionately convinced that it was good for us. Not only did we put the Mentholatum *in* our noses, but we were commanded to "Inhale! Inhale! Get it way down in your lungs where it does the most good . . . like *this!*" and he'd give us a demonstration of snorting in reverse.

Not only do I think of my father whenever I see a jar or tube of Mentholatum, but the muscles of my throat contract in a stimulus-response reaction to the days when I almost strangled on the stuff every night. The Mentholatum season began in October, which Papa termed "the month of drafts," and continued through March. Once started, we engaged in a nightly routine at bedtime. Thoroughly smeared and greased, we "took off" from the warmth of the back sitting room to the iciness of the sleeping porch. This open-air boudoir was Papa's idea. In January and February it was more a refrigerator than a room. Indeed, it was as near to the Great Outdoors as any room could get.

Papa built the sleeping porch so we'd all have "lots and lots of fresh air." We did. Lots and lots. The porch was huge. On it was a double bed for each of the four children, one for Mama, and one for Papa. There were no walls at all—not if you thought of a wall as a solid surface. The three exposed sides of the porch consisted of windows adjoining windows all the way around. Only screens were between us and Nature. They kept the flies and mosquitoes out in summer, but merely added insult to injury in the winter.

To be sure, there were panes. Each window had them.

But the panes "disappeared." "Look!" Papa said joyfully as he conducted visitors on the grand tour of the house on Oak Street. "Disappearing windows! *Both* panes lower all the way down to the sill!" He then hastened to add that the only time both panes came out of hiding was when it rained in. In the summertime the disappearing windows allowed the maximum amount of breeze to come in. While they came up for rain, they stayed down for snow. "Nothing like pure, clean snow on top of the feather beds!" Papa said. It didn't snow often in Oklahoma, but when it did, we slept in it. Papa said it was good for us.

I still shiver when I recall the sensation of sliding into that ice-cold bed after the dash from the back sitting room. On second thought, we didn't slide. We jumped. We landed with a shock and lay numbly under our feather beds. Our feet were chunks of ice between the gelid sheets. We drew ourselves up into embryonic balls, waiting for our bodies to warm the bedclothes. From these cocoon positions we lowered our legs gingerly toward the foot of the bed, an inch at a time, nursing what little warmth we had captured, deploying ourselves finally to full length. Then, just as we began to breath normally and to feel cozy and relaxed, with our mentholated noses barely protruding from the covers, onto the porch stalked Papa to take his nightly inventory. He went from bed to bed feeling our feet. If he decided that anyone's feet were too cold, he'd wedge a pillow under them to warm them up. This was a jolly gesture of good will inasmuch as the pillow itself was freezing cold. Then, like a football coach, he patted us affectionately and shouted words of encouragement and advice about bed manners. One of his most important maxims was Don't Sleep on Your Heart.

"Turn over on your right side, Son. You're sleepin' on your heart."

"Please, Papa, let me turn over after a while. I'll turn when the bed gets warmer. I *promise* I will."

"Do you want to strain your heart, Son?" He was using that convincing voice of his which turned night into day and black into white. "My boy, it's just because I love you so much that I want you to sleep on your right side. I don't want you burdenin' your little heart."

Yielding to the inevitable, I'd roll over—envying the man I'd read about whose heart was on his right side and who, on Papa's sleeping porch, would therefore be permitted to sleep on his left side all night long.

As my sisters grew older they insisted upon, and got, their own bedrooms indoors. They slept on whichever side they pleased and they lowered their *non*disappearing windows no more than one inch from the top.

My mother remained on the porch, but she stayed on her own terms. Once Papa insisted that Manny roll over on his right side and that I roll over on mine. He then bent over Mama's bed and whispered very softly into her ear, "Annie darling, you're on the wrong side. Turn over on your right side. You're sleepin' on your heart."

Mama burrowed deeper into her feather bed, held firmly to her entrenched position, and said sleepily, "Max darling, you can go to hell. I'm not moving."

Papa didn't think it was funny when she said it, but for many years—even after Mama had died—he told the story on himself at family gatherings. As he told it, the past caught up with the present. His laughter trailed away. He said, "Your mother was a wonderful woman. She never crossed me very often. She almost always let me have my own way." That was his own way of saying he loved her.

If Papa was fond of Mentholatum, he had a passionate love affair with Epsom salts. He said he could cure anything with it, and he certainly tried. If you sprained an ankle or wrist, you simply bathed it repeatedly in warm solutions of Epsom salts and it felt just like new in no time! Ingrown toenails, athlete's foot, rashes, fallen arches, boils, and rheumatism responded to the "exterior" Epsom salts treatment. The "interior" prescription applied to everything from arthritis to zinc poisoning. It was common knowledge throughout the entire state of Oklahoma that if you were foolish enough to complain about your health to Max Meyer you got what you deserved: a tall tumbler filled to the brim with warm, colorless, acrid Epsom salts.

Papa believed so fervently in the healing powers of Epsom salts that he literally hypnotized reluctant prospects into drinking down the bitter liquid to the last drop. "Don't stop now! Don't stop now!" he'd yell as the victim started to drink. "Drink it all! Keep goin'!" If he had had it in his power, Papa would have made this magical, marvelous cleanser and cure-all legal tender. Why *not* an Epsom, instead of a gold, standard?

He bought Epsom salts in twenty-five- and fifty-pound sacks. He made fresh batches of solutions periodically, storing it in gallon jugs. His favorite prescription was "a light dose of salts every mornin' for seven days." This is what he referred to as "the course." Anyone who took the course "couldn't help feelin' happier and healthier when it was over." Lighter, too!

Papa even convinced Mama that Epsom salts was good for "tonin' up the system." She took the course at least twice a year. I took the course, too, along with the other children. It was one thing that got no easier with practice. I could never distinguish between a "light" dose and a "heavy" one. I loathed the taste of Epsom salts. I also loathed the sweet preserves Papa had waiting on a spoon afterward to "take the taste away." Invariably, it was preserves that my mother had made years before and forgotten about. Papa discovered it in a dark spot of the cellar and brought it upstairs. Oversweet, grainy with sugar, it was awful. But Papa couldn't stand to see anything halfway edible thrown away, so he used this dreadful sweet stuff as counterirritant to the bitter brew.

Almost as important as the salts itself was what came afterward. Two hours after the dose was downed Papa assailed you with cup after steaming cup of weak, lemonade tea. If you balked, Papa acted hurt. He pleaded, "Without the tea you lose all the benefits! You've come this far; now don't stop. It's the tea that acts as the cleansin' agent."

"Most people are like rusty radiators," Papa said. "They get all clogged up and need a periodic flushin' out."

In all fairness to Papa, let it be said that he took the course himself, as regularly as anyone else. And it must be admitted that his health was uniformly good. Whether it was good because of or in spite of the Epsom salts, only the good Lord knows. I learned from my father that Epsom salts made the skin clearer, the eyes brighter, the hair more lustrous. It stopped gas, heartburn, and clogged digestion. It also had other uses which he merely hinted at—uses reserved for the desperate situations female adults sometimes get themselves into. He never came right out and defined these "other uses," but he seemed to be convinced that they existed.

As a circuit rider takes his Bible to the people, so Papa (who believed that constipation was a sin) took his Epsom salts to all who might benefit from it. Tenants along his WPA Row knew that once every three months Max started out from the Big House in their direction. He strode down the dusty road that led past their front doors. He carried a gallon jug of colorless fluid, swinging it jauntily, his index finger looped through the handle at the bottle's neck. He paused long enough at each house to administer a dose of Epsom salts to every man, woman, and child he found there. Each of the six houses along the Row was overpopulated, tenant-farmer fashion. But Papa was generous. No one was left out. Everybody got his fair share of the vile liquid and the frightful preserves.

One day, after we had moved to the ranch permanently, Judge Wright drove out from town for a visit. When I told him that Papa was over yonder giving Epsom salts to all his tenant farmers, the Judge was stunned.

"Max!" he said the moment Papa reappeared, swinging his nearly empty jug. "The boy here tells me that . . . he says that you . . . that these poor people . . . men, women, and helpless little children are forced to . . . Do you mean to say that they *let* you do this thing to them?"

Papa looked supremely happy. "They know from experience that it works, Judge. Nothing like a course of Epsom salts to tone up the whole system. The men work better afterward and the women are less tired. Helps the children, too. Quiets 'em down."

"What about them right now?" Judge Wright asked innocently. "Aren't they *sick* from it?"

"Oh, my God, no!" Papa said. "You oughta see 'em runnin' out those back doors. They're passin' each other comin' and goin'. They'll be all right by tomorrow. I gave each household a half-dozen lemons and a package of tea. It's the hot lemonade tea afterward that does the trick."

Judge Wright gasped. He rose from his chair and shook his finger at Papa. "Max! You'd better be careful. You'll have a fine lawsuit slapped on you some day for dosing innocent people with Epsom salts."

"You're talkin' crazy, Judge," Papa replied, grinning, "and I've just been thinkin' that *you* look a little peaked yourself. I've got enough left in this jug for one more dose!"

The Judge didn't answer. He was in his car, out of the driveway, and onto the highway in nothing flat.

When I found Papa alone in the room, I asked, "Where's Judge Wright? I thought he'd stay and have lunch with us."

"He had to run," Papa said, laughing.

Papa ignored hospitals for the first seventy-six years of his life. When he finally landed in one it was because he was too sick to protest.

He was suspicious of hospitals. Once I caught him spitting surreptitiously as he drove by one. He looked sheepish when I asked him what he was doing. I'm certain that when he was alone in a car he *always* spat as he passed a hospital. He was superstitious about such places, and he practiced his own brand of black magic to protect himself from them.

Although he refused to enter hospitals, no one could accuse him of being thoughtless of sick people. Papa spent hours in front of greeting-card racks, selecting get-well messages which he sent to friends, relatives, friends of friends, relatives of relatives, and total strangers he read about in the papers.

If one of his own children was hospitalized, he made the supreme effort of visiting the child once—and only once—during his or her sojourn. When a grandchild was born, Papa dashed inside the hospital, visited the new mother for one minute, gazed at the new grandbaby through the glass, and scooted. "It just *does* something to me when I get inside a hospital," he said many times. "Don't ever put me in one of those places. I'll never come out alive."

We finally had to put him in one. He not only came out alive. He made medical history!

The telephone rang at five o'clock on a Sunday morning.

"Sonny?"

"Hello, Papa."

"Did I wake you up?"

"Yes," I said sleepily. "That's all right. Is something the matter?"

"I think I'm sick."

I was awake now. "Tell me."

"It's my stomach. It's been painin' me somethin' awful. I wanted to wait till you were up before I called but I can't stand this much longer."

"Maybe Jeanette had better call a doctor," I said, knowing Papa would never call one for himself.

"Jeanette's in Kansas City," Papa said. "She left yesterday. Her sister's sick."

"Get in bed and stay there," I told him, "and *don't take any Epsom salts.* I'll bring a doctor from Tulsa to look you over just as soon as I can locate one."

As soon as Papa had said good-by I called the one doctor who could handle him, Dr. David Graham. Dr. Graham combined brilliance in surgery with plenty of old-fashioned homespun folksiness. "Doctor," I said, "I'm sorry to get you out of bed, but something's wrong with my father. Will you drive out to our ranch with me? I'd bring him to you but I think he's too sick to be moved."

"Let's go," Dr. Graham answered immediately. "I'll be ready by the time you get here."

Within an hour the doctor was inspecting Papa. I remained a discreet distance away, respecting my father's innate modesty where the naked body was concerned. I could tell that he was sicker than he'd ever been before.

"Right through here, Doc," he kept saying, pointing to the vast expanse of stomach under the sheet. "Hurts like hell."

Dr. Graham poked and probed, then walked into the next room to talk to me. "He's got to be moved to a hospital, and quickly. I'll call and reserve a room. The trouble could be his appendix. It could be his liver. It could be worse. What's his past medical record? He won't volunteer a thing."

"He doesn't *have* any," I said. "He was shot once when he was young. I think he was shot in the rear, but I'm not sure where nor how. He was in some sort of scrape at the time and he only hints at what happened."

The doctor returned to Papa's bed. "Tell me about your injury . . . the time you were shot. Show me where."

"Oh, Doc, that was sixty years ago and more. I was a punk kid in Hot Springs, Arkansas, and we were doin' something we shouldn't have been doin'. It was Halloween. Somebody shot my whole ass full of buckshot. I was full of it. Old Doc Cassidy took it out of me. . . . Ever know Doc Cassidy at Hot Springs? Wonderful man! . . . Well, old Doc Cassidy patched me up—down here." Papa lifted the sheet, pointed, let the doctor look briefly, and then dropped it again. "He said I could've been ruined for life. You know. No kids. I was plenty lucky." When he said "lucky" he knocked on the wood headboard of the bed. He wasn't too sick to be taking chances.

"Darned good job of patching up!" Dr. Graham said. "It's held perfectly for a mighty long time."

Sixty years and more. Those words of Papa's hit me with an impact. Papa was old. None of us had thought about his being old because he was always breathing fire and raising Cain. Now, lying here quietly, without any fight, he almost seemed his age.

"Papa," I ventured timidly, "I've called the ambulance. We're going to take you to the hospital in Tulsa."

"The hell you say."

"Now, Papa—"

"I ain't goin'. Doc can do what he has to do to me right here."

"He's going to run tests, Papa. He can't find out what's wrong with you out here on the ranch. He's agreed to drive my car back to Tulsa, and I'm going in the ambulance with you."

"Son," Papa said, "you know I don't like to ride in . . . in . . . *them things*. Can't I pull my trousers on and kinda lean on the back seat of your car?"

Dr. Graham heard this and shook his head. "Mr. Meyer, you're not going to ride in a *hearse*."

At the sound of that word Papa shuddered, spat, and knocked wood three times.

"It's an *ambulance*," Dr. Graham continued. "I promise you that you'll be coming home in your own front seat."

"Call the thing," Papa groaned. He was hurting too much to protest. If he had felt like arguing, he'd have won his point.

Papa was certain he'd never come back alive. To ease the tension I tried to joke a bit with the driver, a kid of nineteen or twenty. "My father's a terrible back-seat driver," I said.

"Just take it easy, Mr. Meyer," the boy said. "You don't know me, but you know my uncle. I'm Gus Taylor's nephew."

Papa nodded his head. He was too sick to tell the dozen or more stories he ordinarily would have told about Gus

Taylor, who owned the Farmer's Exchange, a place where Papa met his friends and ate his lunches (in the fresh produce department).

The young driver was proud of his passenger. Papa was small-town royalty. The boy kept the car's temperature constant, spoke very little, watched the road carefully, and used body English to ease every bump and jar.

"Look, Son," Papa said to me as we drove along in the ambulance. "Your mother was the finest person I ever knew. I loved her with all my heart."

"I know, Papa."

"Jeanette's a mighty sweet woman and I love her, too. She's taken good care of your old Dad for almost ten years, and somebody's gonna have to look after her."

"For Pete's sake, Papa, stop that kind of talk! You're going to be all right. You'll be taking care of Jeanette yourself for a long, long time."

Papa shook his head, as though he knew better.

"About the ranch," he said. "Don't let people buy it in pieces. Keep it all together. Find one person who has a bunch of cattle to run and sell it to him all in one piece."

"Nobody's selling the ranch!" I protested. "If you don't stop that kind of conversation, Papa, I'm going to sit up front with Gus Taylor's nephew and leave you here alone!"

He quieted down. I reached over and took one of his huge, sun-browned hands and held it until the ambulance pulled up to the special entrance. Two orderlies helped the driver and me get Papa settled in the room Dr. Graham had arranged for.

Papa looked far too big for the bed. Despite his antipathy

to anything remotely connected with a hospital, the novelty of being in a bed with a half-dozen people dancing attendance was not displeasing to him.

What happened next, happened quickly.

"We're going to operate in an hour," Dr. Graham said to me. "I'm afraid to wait. This could be something serious. I don't say this to frighten you. I feel you ought to know."

"I've got a favor to ask, Doctor. Will *you* tell him about the operation? I don't think I'm up to it."

I stayed in the hall while the doctor went in. I was braced for an eruption. Instead, I heard Papa say in a weak voice which still had his kidding tone, "My last major operation was seventy-six years ago, Doc. The rabbi performed it nine days after I was born. Hope your job turns out half as good."

Dr. Graham passed me in a hurry. He didn't want to look at me, and I knew why.

Five minutes later Papa was saying to me, "I want you kids to get along with each other. I don't want you to hold grudges."

"Yes, Papa."

"The building on North Main is well built. When you sell it make 'em pay what it's worth. It has a basement that's as dry as a bone. I wouldn't want anyone to steal that building from you all, Son."

"Nobody's stealing anything, Papa! You're going to be *all right!*"

"Don't sell the old store building Grandpa Philip Levy

gave me. It's still the best location in town. It'll always rent for good money."

"If you only knew how silly you sound, Papa."

"Keep the others out of the hospital until tomorrow. . . ."

"Yes, Papa. Here they come. . . ."

The orderlies transferred him from his bed to a cart on wheels. They wheeled him down the hall toward the operating room. He reached out his hand and I grasped it.

"We'll all say a prayer for you, Papa," I said. I knew he was thinking along those lines.

As they started pushing Papa into the operating room, he asked them to stop the cart. He motioned me to him.

"Sonny boy . . . get in touch with that nice little Orthodox rabbi. Remember. The *Orthodox* one. I won't understand what he's sayin' but I'll feel better with him around."

"Now, Papa—"

"The little *Orthodox* . . . one! Don't . . . forget!"

He'd had the last word.

Dr. Graham was tired and jubilant when he shook me awake and said, "Your Dad's going to be O.K. Largest gall bladder anyone around here ever saw—thirteen inches long. Way over a thousand gallstones! I've got two people counting them now. He'll want to know exactly how many . . . Miracle we got to it when we did. Miracle. Nothing you can do here. Go to bed. And don't thank me. I never had a better patient. I'll never forget your Papa."

It couldn't be happening! Papa was having the time of his life—and in a hospital! He relished the flowers. He displayed the dozens of cards and letters he received. He complained only mildly about the expense of his three special nurses. Once he was convinced that he was going to live through it, he played the role of patient to the hilt. Jeanette, who had returned from Kansas City to be with him, didn't dare stray more than a few feet from his room. All four children had to check in and out at regular intervals. His daughter-in-law sent special dishes for his trays twice a day. His grandchildren called on the telephone. Visitors from all over Oklahoma — people his family had never seen but whom Papa knew intimately — crowded into his room to shake his hand and tell him to hurry home.

What pleased him most was when doctors dropped in just to see this "new page in the Journal." Papa grinned and said, "One thousand, five hundred and sixty-six gallstones, gentlemen! . . . Here, have some candy. . . . Bladder was twelve and a half inches long!" He sacrificed a precious half-inch rather than use the dreaded word "thirteen." ". . . Sit down! Help yourselves to some cake. . . . Ask Doc Graham if you don't believe me. One thousand, five hundred and sixty-six stones. He counted 'em!" The more they marveled, the more he beamed.

When he returned home it was in his own front seat.

11. THE HOUSE ON CEDAR STREET

Papa loved to talk about the weather. He loved to quote statistics. "Did you know that Oklahoma has more days of sunshine than any other state in the Union?"

After hearing him ask this question all of my life, I inquired one day, "How many days of sunshine *does* Oklahoma average each year?"

"Search me," Papa said.

"You mean you make up that business about Oklahoma's being the sunshiniest state in the Union?"

"Not exactly," he mused. "Seems to me like I heard some authority say it once. We *do* have a lot of sunshine here, and it's time someone put in a plug for our climate. Ever since Will Rogers told people to wait a minute if they didn't like the Oklahoma weather, we've taken an awful beatin'. Our weather is wonderful! The winters are warm—"

193

"And the summers are warmer," I reminded him.

"Yes, but that hot, dry weather is healthy weather. The hotter it gets, the healthier people are! Hardly anybody gets sick in the summertime."

Although he called it "the month of drafts," October was Papa's favorite month of the year. October days are warm in Oklahoma but not uncomfortably hot. October nights are pleasantly cool. The golden haze of the early fall days was enclosed in a picture frame of red and yellow leaves on the scrub oaks, the green of the grass, and the always surprising abundance of late roses in bloom.

Papa could carry on for hours about the blueness of Oklahoma sky in October. He'd stand on the sidewalk in front of the Farmer's Exchange studying the sky until someone would walk up and say, "Whatcha lookin' at, Max?"

"Just admirin' the sky," Papa'd answer. "Oklahoma has the bluest blue sky in the world."

Curiously conscious of the sky as sky for the first time in his life, the friend would look too.

"It's blue all right, Max. Blue as hell."

"Know why it's such a blue blue?" Papa would ask. "It's the *air* makes it blue. See how clear the air is? Breathe it! Go on. *Breathe* it!" He'd fill his lungs with air so delicious he'd have to close his eyes to stand the pure joy of tasting it. "Better'n wine," he'd exhale. "Pure champagne!"

The friend would inhale some champagne and nod his head in agreement.

"Gives me an appetite," Papa would add, coming down to earth. "Let's go over here, and I'll treat you to a banana."

It was just such a clear, blue October day that Papa got the house-moving fever.

I was in my office, tilted back in the swivel chair, from which position I could waste time pleasantly looking out of the window to see who was going into the post office, when I heard Papa coming down the hall. He didn't just walk when he was bursting with an idea. He reverberated. You could hear him half a floor away. The glass panes in the lawbook cases trembled as he stamped into the room. He kissed me, smiled, and said, "Hello, Sonny boy."

His flushed face and the sparks his eyes sent out gave him away. He had something to tell. But first he said, "You oughta be wearin' a jacket, Son. It's too cool for shirt sleeves. It's not summer."

"Take a look at yourself, Papa. You're wearing a short-sleeved sport shirt."

"I've been out in the sun where it's warm," he countered. "It's too cool indoors to be without something on your shoulders."

"Too *hot* or too *cool?*" I asked out of mischief. Papa made a face. He didn't think that was funny. He sat down on the other side of the desk from me, picked up a pencil, and started drawing squares and triangles on a piece of foolscap.

"It's like this," he began, intent on his doodling. "All you have to do is give me twelve hundred dollars now. I'll give you four times that much as soon as we get the house moved and sold."

"What house?" I asked.

"Why," Papa began patiently, as though I should have

known all the time, "that little white house on Cedar Street. The house your Mama and I lived in when we first moved to Sapulpa."

"What about it?" I asked.

"What *about* it? Why, they were gonna tear it *down*," Papa replied indignantly. "*That's* what about it! They're gonna build a new Safeway Store on that corner and they were all set to tear the house down and sell it for salvage when I took it off their hands."

I sat up so quickly the swivel chair whacked me in the small of the back. "You took it . . . off their . . . *hands?*"

"Yep," Papa said proudly, drawing triangles inside the triangles. "I said I'd buy the house and move it myself. They originally wanted two thousand dollars for it, but I got 'em down to twelve hundred dollars—cash."

I opened my mouth but Papa grabbed my word away from me.

"Now, Sonny, you know that you don't want that house torn down any more than I do. It's—it's *symbolic*. Your mother and I spent our first happy months of married life in that little house. Why, your own sister Beatrice was—was"—his modesty checked him—"was *decided on* right there in the little bedroom." He looked up from his scribbles. "If you don't mind, you can write me out a check for twelve hundred dollars and I'll start makin' the arrangements to move it. It's gotta be off there by Saturday."

"You don't know the first thing about moving a house, Papa," I said, stalling for time, trying to get my counterattack going. "You don't have any idea what you're getting into. And where in heaven's name will you move it?"

"Leave that to me, Sonny. Just write out the check. I've already got everything planned. I'm gonna move the house from its corner on Cedar Street to the lot I own on East Dewey Avenue. It's a little house. Only four rooms and a small porch. Easy as pie to move it with a big truck. I'll take it all the way down Dewey Avenue late Thursday night and have it on the new lot by Friday mornin'. Hurry up and write out the check. I don't want the Safeway people to think I've changed my mind. Twelve hundred dollars is a giveaway for that nice house. It'll bring fifty-five hundred—six thousand when I get it moved. Just think of all that profit!"

All that profit! A few weeks later, when I was posting the canceled check for twelve hundred dollars in the family ledger, I saw that Papa had been in such a hurry to get his hands on the money that he had smudged the still-wet ink on the date line as he snatched the check and ran.

All that profit! With hindsight instead of foresight, it was easy to see all the things Papa hadn't considered in his project. A stack of canceled checks told the story in full: the cost of the new foundation and the rebuilding of a new porch; the cost of replastering, repainting, and repapering all four rooms; the price of new plumbing and kitchen pipes and fixtures; the complete reflooring of the house (during the move, something happened to make the floors buckle); and the construction of a driveway and carport. One canceled check was made payable to "Frank L. Bronson" in the sum of five hundred dollars, with the notation "In full payment of sideswiping costs when my house tore a hole in your bedroom." My hand trembled as I picked up a check for $650 annotated "In full settlement of all legal claims that Max Meyer deposited a house on four feet of your lot."

All that profit! There was no check for a fine, although a fine had been levied against Papa for obstructing traffic and committing a public nuisance. Papa refused to pay it, arguing that what happened was "an act of God." Eventually he talked the City Commission into suspending it.

But let me fill in the details of how "the house on Cedar Street" was transformed into "the house on Dewey Avenue." Papa's cup of joy spilled over. Now that the house belonged to him, all he had to do was relocate it.

He drove to the ranch and got Ernie, the pickup, and the two Indians. Ernie drove. Papa sat in the front seat. The Indians squatted on the bed of the pickup. When they got to Cedar Street they all got out and studied the job to be done.

"I'll rent a big truck," Papa said. "A Mack Super. We'll jack the house up, move it to the new lot, jack it up again when we get there, and Ern can build a new brick foundation under it while it's up in the air."

"Maybe I oughta go over to the new lot and start a foundation now so's we can kinda ease the house onto it?" Ernie suggested.

"Ain't time," Papa answered. "The Safeway folks have to have the lot all cleared by Saturday. Today's Wednesday. We've gotta get 'er ready to go by tomorrow night. We'll borrow the jacks from the county engineer, rent the truck, and located some sort of trailer to move the house on."

Happy as larks, Papa and his crew went about their errands, borrowing jacks, renting a truck, fetching rope. They lined up everything except a trailer. They couldn't locate one. They even drove to Tulsa and looked without any luck.

"We've gotta put the house on some sort of wheels to move it," Papa said. "There isn't a dolly or trailer anywhere." He looked discouraged.

Big Indian pulled at Papa's sleeve. "You don't need a trailer," he said. "All you need are two long poles. Like telephone poles. We'll tie the poles to the truck, put the house on the poles, and let the poles drag on the ground, Indian-style."

It was the longest speech Papa had ever heard Big Indian make. "Indian-style?" Papa asked.

"Yep. Indians moved bigger things than that little house on pole shafts drawn by horses. It's called a travois."

Papa was pleased beyond words at Big Indian's brilliance. "Well!" he said, relieved. "Telephone poles! Now that's more *like* it."

All day Thursday they worked on the house. The Indians started jacking up the house and moving the telephone poles in place beneath it. Papa drove Ernie to get the Mack Super. While Ernie was driving the truck back to Cedar Street, Papa dropped in at the police station.

"Hi, Max. What can I do for you?" Sergeant Mosey said pleasantly.

"Nothing at all, Mo," Papa said. "I just thought I'd tell you that I'm movin' a house from Cedar Street to a lot I own on East Dewey Avenue tonight, so's you'd already know about it if anyone mentioned it to you."

Sergeant Mosey shot out of his chair. "You're moving a house your*self*, Max?"

"Oh, I've got my crew helpin' me. It's all ready to go."

Sergeant Mosey wrinkled his forehead. He'd heard about Papa's locomotive. "May I inquire, Max, what route you plan to take with your house?"

"We're gonna drag it one block south on Cedar Street to Dewey Avenue, and then proceed due east on Dewey through town to the new lot."

"Max, you can't do that! Dewey Avenue is Highway 66. I can't let you block Highway 66 with a house."

Papa looked at Sergeant Mosey with disbelief. "Mo, I'm surprised at your attitude. You know very well that I personally voted twenty-three people from my ranch for your Uncle Frank when he ran for Sheriff. He won by exactly ten votes, remember? You're also aware that your father and I started the first Boy Scout Camp in Creek County thirty years ago. I've never asked you for a favor in my life. I happened to drop in to tell you what I'm gonna do and you start puttin' obstacles in my way. Now, Mo, the shortest distance between the old lot and the new lot is right down Dewey Avenue, and you know it. It wouldn't hurt you and one of the other cops to direct the traffic a block west while we're goin' down Dewey . . . but you don't have to if you don't want to. We'll manage O.K. without you. We'll start around four tomorrow morning. We'll have the house on the new lot by six. There won't be two dozen cars that'll have to detour that early. Now what's so awful about that?"

Sergeant Mosey surrendered. "Have it your way, Max. Me and the boys will be at the corner of Dewey and Cedar at four A.M." He groaned. "O-o-oh! I just remembered. Tomorrow afternoon's the parade."

"Parade?"

"Tomorrow night's the football game between Sapulpa and Bristow. The whole force has to work the game to prevent another gang fight like they had last year. They decided to have a parade this year so's both sides could let off steam in advance. There'll be bands and floats and . . ." His voice trailed away. "Max, couldn't you please, as a personal favor to me, move your house Sunday morning?"

"Can't do it, Mo. Has to be off the lot by Saturday. That's part of the deal. Don't worry. I'll take care of the house part. You get to bed early tonight and get your rest."

Sergeant Mosey looked whipped. "Tonight's my anniversary and I'm taking my wife to Tulsa to a show. We won't get home till one o'clock. You start moving your house at four. The parade starts at noon. The game's tomorrow night. *What* rest?"

Papa edged toward the door before Sergeant Mosey changed his mind. He was almost outside before he remembered the occasion. "Happy anniversary, Mo!" Papa yelled heartily, then shut the door behind him in a hurry.

Sergeant Mosey folded his arms on his desk and leaned his head down on them. For a few moments he stayed that way, quietly hating his Uncle Frank and every Boy Scout in Creek County.

The house looked frail and helpless perched on the pronged poles behind the truck. It would take its ride hindside to, its back wall hoisted up against the truck, its little front porch at the lower end of the tilt. There was something wistful about the way it faced its abandoned foundation. The Indians had tied the poles to the truck and the house to the poles with lines of rope. Everything was set.

"Nothing to do till we start the move," Papa said. Ernie announced that he'd walk over to his brother-in-law's house, sleep there, and meet them at the lot early in the morning. Little Indian drove the pickup back to the ranch with Papa wedged in between him and Big Indian.

Papa went to bed right after supper, but slept badly. He was nervous about the house. He got up at two, dressed, and read the paper until the Indians came to the Big House a little after three. He warmed over some coffee that was left in the percolator and poured the Indians and himself a cup. The hot, bitter stuff did, at least, wake them all up. Neither Papa nor the Indians spoke a word as they drove toward Cedar Street. It was chilly but not cold—still summery weather in October.

Ernie was perched on the front bumper of the Mack Super waiting for them. He had evidently waited through the two empty pint bottles on the ground by the truck.

"G'mornin'," he said thickly. He was squiffled, plastered, stoned, embalmed.

Papa was furious at himself for not taking into account Ernie's proclivity for escape. He studied Ernie, trying to decide what to do with him.

Ernie made the decision for him. "Brother-'n-law wasn't 'ome," he explained earnestly, and passed out, his head falling cozily between the headlight and the radiator of the Mack Super.

"You'll have to be the driver, Little Indian," Papa said.

"What'll we do with him?" Big Indian asked, pointing at the sprawling, snoring Ernie, who was still perched on the truck's bumper.

"We could leave him in the pickup here, but I'm afraid he'll go for more liquor when he wakes up," Papa said.

"Why don't we take him with us? That way he won't get into a lot of trouble."

The three of them carried Ernie to the little house and deposited him on the floor of what had been the front bedroom. They wedged him against the wall at the foot of the tilt, so he wouldn't roll around too much during the journey. "We can keep an eye on him this way," Papa said.

Little Indian started up the truck, shifted gears, and eased it slowly toward the street. The house groaned, but rode its poles snugly, even during the ticklish drop from the curb onto the street. Papa didn't look back until they were turning off Cedar onto Dewey Avenue. He asked Little Indian to stop the truck for a minute so he could get out. He took a few steps back down the empty street toward the street light at the corner. The old lot looked strange with the house gone. He stood there for a few seconds, then turned around and walked quickly back to the truck with the house on its back.

"Let 'er rip!" Papa commanded.

Little Indian let 'er rip, not only managing the difficult left turn onto Dewey Avenue from Cedar Street, but managing with one of the protruding poles to smash a hole in the side of a frame home that protruded two feet too far for its own good. The splintering, cracking noises were followed almost immediately by loud and profuse swearing on the part of the owner, who had been sound asleep in his own bed when the moving house assaulted him. The man was as frightened as he was angry when he came charging out of the front door. He was also stark-naked, which didn't seem to slow him down much.

Papa led the man back inside his house and assured him that he'd stand the expenses of repairing the torn corner. Papa told him how sorry he was, got him back to bed again, and returned to the truck. "For Pete's sake, take it easy!" Papa said to Little Indian as they started what proved to be a historic ride down Dewey Avenue.

The block before Dewey Avenue crosses Main Street is a steep incline. At the foot of this hill, where Main Street and Dewey intersect, was Sapulpa's only traffic light. Main Street becomes Highway 75, which leads to Dallas. Dewey is Highway 66, to California. It is an important corner. If the traffic light had not changed to red when it did, and if Papa hadn't startled sleepy Little Indian who was driving the truck down the hill, nothing at all would have happened. But the light did change, and Papa did shout, and all hell broke loose.

The signal light showed green as the truck began to descend the grade. With the weight of the house behind it, the Mack Super gained momentum as it went down the hill. It hadn't occurred to Little Indian to stop at the signal. The whole town was deserted. There wasn't a car coming up Dewey or going down Main as far as anybody could see. Who ever heard of a traffic cop on the prowl at four A.M.? Besides, moving a house, he felt, gave you certain privileges. As the light turned amber, Little Indian kept right on going.

But to Papa a red light was as red at predawn as it was at high noon.

"Stop the truck! Stop it . . . *stop* it!" Papa screamed.

Little Indian slammed his foot on the brake the way you'd stamp on a running spider. The brakes began to screech, the truck began to skid to one side. If the house hadn't been supported on its back, the Mack Super would have stopped properly at the red light. Instead of stopping, however, the truck and its cargo swayed wildly, popping the ropes that were tied to one end of the travois, and sending that particular telephone pole out from under the house at a right angle to the truck. When the truck finally stopped, the house was smack in the middle of Sapulpa's number one intersection, with one end of the lopsided front porch still tied to its pole and the other end resting uncomfortably on the street.

Papa was surveying the damage when Sergeant Mosey and one of his patrolmen appeared.

"Hello, Mo," Papa said cheerfully. "I don't think the house is hurt at all. The pole holdin' this side of it just scooted right out from under."

It might have been the color of the early morning sky. It might have been his short sleep. But Sergeant Mosey looked pale green. "Max—" he began. "I told you, Max—" He didn't finish. He couldn't get the words out. Far down Dewey Avenue a car was headed toward them. Sergeant Mosey turned to his patrolman. "Don't just *stand* there, Al! Set up a roadblock and detour traffic around us or we'll have a pile-up that'll never get untangled!" He headed for the patrol car to call for help on the short-wave radio. In his mind he was figuring out where he'd have to set up detour signs on Main Street and at the top of the hill on Dewey. He'd have to work fast, and he couldn't count on help until the other officers got out of bed and got dressed.

"Don't get excited, Mo," Papa said calmly. "Easy does it."

Mo's nerves exploded. He began to shout at the top of his lungs. "Damn it all, Max Meyer. I'm gonna throw the book at you. You're gonna pay the biggest fine in the history of Creek County—for obstructing traffic and for operating a public nuisance. I *told* you what would happen, didn't I? You're the craziest, stubbornest hammerhead in the U.S.A.!"

Papa was hurt; but Ernie, who had been jarred awake by the bump when the pole skidded out from under his bedroom, was infuriated. He crawled across the room on his hands and knees, stuck his head out of what had been the bedroom window, and said to Sergeant Mosey, "Don't you talk to Max like that, you crazy damn fool you." Pulling himself up from the floor, Ernie half fell out of the window as he wagged his finger at the officer and shouted insultingly, "Crazy hammerhead your*self!* Hammerhead! Hammerhead! Hammerhead! HAMMERHEAD!"

Sergeant Mosey went insane. He leaped for Ernie as a tackle dives for a ball carrier. He grabbed Ernie under the armpits and pulled him out of the window before Ernie knew what was happening to him. He half dragged, half pulled, half carried the limber Ernie to the police car, dumped him into the back seat, started the siren full blast, and headed for the jail. He tried to proceed straight down Dewey by squeezing past the front of the truck, but he couldn't make it, ripping his fender on a lamp post in the process.

In a spinning of wheels and racing of motor he backed up, sped a block down Main Street, turned left on two wheels, then left again at the next corner until he got back on Dewey Avenue, then headed hellbent for the courthouse. "Be back in a minute!" he yelled at his detour-directing patrolman, Al. Al couldn't imagine why Mo was racing down the street with his siren blasting the dawn. Al couldn't see Mo's hapless prisoner, who was doomed to spend the largest part of that hectic night rolling around on strange and sundry floors that never stopped bouncing.

The Sapulpa National Bank, on the corner of Main and Dewey, opens for business at nine o'clock in the morning. That Friday morning was no exception. The doors opened at nine, as usual, but it was a few minutes after the hour before the first customers could get inside. All streets surrounding the bank were closed to traffic, and those who made it came by foot. Many who emerged from the bank lingered on the corner to stare at the frame house huddled in the midst of the intersection, tilted to one side like an animal with a broken leg. Indeed, the telephone pole which had slipped to such a crazy angle looked *exactly* like a broken leg. The traffic signal light kept changing from red to green over the house's rooftop, like a protective beacon.

Papa knew most of the crowd by their first names and circulated freely among them. Instead of being embarrassed by the turn of events, he seemed radiantly alive and happy.

"How'd it happen, Max?"

"Ropes broke when we stopped at the light."

"Gonna be hard to fix?"

"Naw. Big Indian's gone to the County Barn to borrow two extra-sized jacks. They keep banker's hours over there —don't open up till nine A.M. All we have to do is jack up this end of the house, slip the pole back underneath it, tie it up good and tight, and we're on our way."

Papa saw Sergeant Mosey walking up to him. Papa turned his head and spat. It was not a contemptuous spit but a protective one. Sergeant Mosey was a symbol of disaster to Papa. Without knowing why, Papa blamed all the bad luck on the Sergeant.

"Hello, Max."

"Hello, Mo."

"I've got the entire force detouring traffic over to Lee Street. It's going smooth now."

"That's nice."

"Have you had anything to eat, Max? Any coffee?"

"Nope. Stayed right here with the house."

Sergeant Mosey motioned to Little Indian to come to him. "Go over to the squad car and tell them I told you to bring a thermos of hot coffee here for Max."

Little Indian looked at Papa to see if it was all right to go to the squad car. Papa nodded his O.K.

"Max," Sergeant Mosey began, "I don't want you to be mad at me about last night. I lost my temper and I came here man to man this morning to tell you that I'm sorry."

That was the kind of talk that made Papa melt. He was touched. He held out his huge paw to the Sergeant, who did look dog-tired from all his running around.

Little Indian handed Papa the thermos. Papa poured a cup of coffee for Little Indian, then filled the top of the thermos with coffee for himself. He blew on it a couple of times to cool it off, then gulped it down thirstily.

"Thanks, Mo," Papa said. "Did you have a nice anniversary? I forgot to ask you this morning."

"Went to Tulsa to a show. Got home kind of late. Here comes your other Indian."

Big Indian set the huge jacks down near the corner of the house and walked over to talk to Little Indian.

"Come here and get some hot coffee!" Papa called to Big Indian. "Then we'll tie the house up again." He smiled at Sergeant Mosey. "We'll be ready to roll by noon."

At the word "noon" a sledge hammer beat on Sergeant Mosey's skull.

"Max! You've got to be cleared out of here *before* noon!"

He pointed up the incline on Dewey Avenue where that morning's wild descent had begun. "The football parade starts forming up there around eleven thirty. The parade starts at twelve noon. This house has to be out of the way by noon. D'y' hear me? Noon! Do you need any help?"

Papa looked at the clock in front of the bank. It was already after ten. "We'll do our best, Mo," Papa said. "And we'll manage fine by ourselves."

How Papa and his house got into the parade was the result of a kind of spontaneous combustion. It was everybody's idea at once. The first to suggest it was the captain of the Bristow Purple Pirates, Bill Hartshorne. Bill's grandfather had bought natural stone from Papa for construction work. He knew Papa, so he didn't hesitate to walk up and ask, "Can I help in some way, Mr. Meyer?"

Papa was supervising the Indians who were tightening the ropes of the travois. He looked at Bill. "You're—you're — Now don't *tell* me! . . . Whose boy *are* you?"

"I'm Mr. Hartshorne's grandson," Bill answered.

"Well, for goodness' sakes!" Papa grinned. "And you've come to Sapulpa to see the football game tonight?"

"I'm going to play in it. I'm the captain of the team."

Papa was impressed. "Looks like the whole town of Bristow's already here to watch you."

"Yes, sir. We got a holiday from school today. Most of the kids are up the hill getting ready for the parade." And then his idea was hatched. "Say, Mr. Meyer, why don't you and the house get in the parade, too?"

"Well, I don't think—" hesitated Papa, out of consideration for Sergeant Mosey's blood pressure.

Bill Hartshorne spied the president of the Pep Club across the street and hollered to him. "Hey, Charley! Let's get Mr. Meyer and the house in the parade!" Charley yelled to somebody else, and that one tossed the idea to somebody else, and in just a minute or two the intersection was crowded with boys and girls from Bristow urging Papa to take part in the parade.

"We'll decorate the porch with purple crepe paper and the Bristow Band Queen can sit alongside him," Bill said. "We'll make the house into a peachy float."

Papa was plainly intrigued. But he had another angle. "I'm from Sapulpa, remember? If the Bristow Band Queen sits on the porch with me, the Sapulpa queen ought to sit there, too. That's only fair play."

Someone went to get the Sapulpa Band Queen to see if she'd sit on the same porch with the Bristow Band Queen. She sent word that she would—if Mr. Meyer sat between them.

Sergeant Mosey heard the commotion in the center of the street and came running. He expected to find a brawl in the making, but discovered, instead, members of both schools decorating Papa's house with streamers. He was stunned. He hadn't thought about having Papa's house in the parade, but now that the idea was taking shape there wasn't anything wrong with it. He observed, too, the spirit of co-operation between the rival students. Last year's fight had been a bloody affair. A joint undertaking like this early in the day set an optimistic note for what might follow at the game that night. Sergeant Mosey gave his blessing to the project. More than that, he went into the Sapulpa National Bank and commandeered three of the red leather barrel chairs that people sat on as they waited to ask for loans. He placed these chairs in a row on the tiny porch for Papa and the two queens.

Since the house was a block ahead of the rest of the units forming for the parade, it was chosen to be the first float. The Sapulpa High School Band, which would lead the parade, was instructed to march down the hill, break formation around the house at the intersection, then reform in front of the house and blare away. Papa, the house, and the two Band Queens would follow the band, with the Pep Clubs, the teams, the coaches, the Bristow Band, and the other floats coming along in that order.

It was almost noon. Hundreds of parents, students, teachers, businessmen, and children of all sizes pressed solidly against the curbs on both sides of Dewey Avenue waiting for the parade to begin. Few wore hats because the sun was warm. Most were in shirt sleeves and sport shirts and summer cottons. A pleasant little breeze blew up occasionally. It was just strong enough to tease the flags out in front of the stores.

As the twelve noon whistle sounded, Little Indian started the engine of the Mack Super. Big Indian sat by his side, arms folded, eyes straight ahead. Papa and the Band Queens took their places on the porch. They faced the Sapulpa High School Band, which was that moment coming down Dewey hill playing to the tune of "On Wisconsin":

On Sapulpa, on Sapulpa,
Get that ball in line. . . .
Take the ball away from Bristow,
Touchdown sure this time . . . rah . . . rah . . . rah . . .
On Sapulpa, on Sapulpa . . .

The band looked sharp in its electric-blue uniforms and white visored caps. The marchers kept right on banging and tooting and blowing as they split into two parts, passed the house on either side, then resumed their marching design at the head of the parade.

As the band stepped out, Little Indian let out the clutch on the Mack Super, and the house resumed its journey.

More than one parade watcher got a "well I'll be damned!" expression on his face when he saw a house being moved in the midst of a football parade—only to discover Papa, with a queen on each side of him, sitting on the pitched porch, waving wildly to spectators on both sides of the street.

Judge Ben Wright, who was walking toward the courthouse when the parade started, happened to glance into the street in time to spy Papa on the porch. "My God," he said out loud. It was more of a gasp than an exclamation. "My God. It's Max."

Papa caught Judge Wright's stunned look and yelled, "Hi, Judge! Folks won't forget *this* parade in a hurry!"

Papa was right. Nobody forgot that parade in a hurry. The score of the game is lost. The teams who played are only blurred memories. But the house on the travois, with two pretty girls and Papa on the front porch facing rearward, will never be forgotten by anyone who saw it.

When the procession passed the courthouse, Papa saw Ernie waving to him from the county jail on the third floor. He and the girls waved back at Ernie and each of the queens threw Ernie a kiss.

How to describe Papa's ride? What to compare it to? Cleopatra in her royal barge on the Cydnus? Marshal Foch leading his troops through the Arc de Triomphe? General MacArthur as he arrived at San Francisco? . . . None of those historic pageants outshone Papa's triumph as he drove down Dewey Avenue in the football parade on that blue October day in Sapulpa, Oklahoma.

This was and would always remain Papa's golden hour. He was the potentate on a kingly throne acknowledging his loving subjects. He was the perennial Oklahoma pioneer, preceded by two full-blooded Indians, the noble race of yesterday, flanked by two representatives of the new, fresh youth of Oklahoma's tomorrow. He was more than a bulky man in a faded sport shirt and torn pants. He was Papa the Terrible; he was Papa the Majestic; he was Papa the Lovable; he was Papa the Earthy; he was Papa the Irascible; he was Papa the Kind; he was Papa the Preposterous.

ABOUT THE AUTHOR

LEWIS MEYER is a lawyer who has found his life work in books. He is a graduate of Dartmouth College ("I drove to college in my own Pierce-Arrow convertible. Now I drive a Ford. I'm happier now.") and the University of Michigan Law School ("That's another story."). He has written seven books and owns his beautiful bookstore. He has appeared many times on national TV and has a television book show of his own (on Tulsa's Channel 6) now entering its fifth uninterrupted decade of continuous airing! "My father always taught his children to work at what makes you happy," Lewis says. "He was preposterous all right, but he always made good sense. I miss him."